Ways with Desserts

BY
THE EDITORS OF TIME-LIFE BOOKS

TIME-LIFE/GEDDES & GROSSET

Contents

Ways with Desserts

HOME COOKING

ISBN 0 7054 2047 7

Printed in Italy.

Ways with Desserts

No one needs a dessert. A fruit tart, a blackberry sorbet, a cheesecake are not likely to appear on any nutritionist's list of essential foods. Indeed, it is easy to obtain all the proteins, carbohydrates, fats and other nutrients required for a healthy diet without ever eating a dessert more complex than a slice of ripe melon. Yet for most people there would be something missing in such a regimen, an unassuaged hunger for the sweet taste, the pleasing aroma, the pretty artifice of a dessert—and the deep, abiding satisfaction it provides.

No other category of food highlights the psychological and aesthetic dimensions of eating so clearly as desserts do. The fresh tang of a strawberry-lemon sauce with strawberry halves provides its own unique delight, as does the quintessential mildness of a soothing custard. There is a gamut of textures to choose from—crunchy, creamy, dense, airy—in tantalizing combination with an even broader range of flavours. And there is diversity of temperature too—what other food room temperature, chilled or frozen?

Be it pastry or pudding, crisp or smooth, icy or hot, the heart of a dessert's appeal is its sweetness. Experiments with newborn babies suggest that humans have an innate predilection for the sweet. Just a few hours after birth, babies express only mild satisfaction at the taste of water, and a slightly acid solution prompts them to screw up their faces. A sugar solution, however, makes them smile—perhaps for the first time.

Desserts are the prime foods of festivity. What

wedding or birthday would be complete without its cake, what Christmas without its pudding? Desserts, in short, make us feel good.

Controlling ingredients

The desires that desserts so abundantly fulfil can be accommodated without compromising the goal of healthy eating. The desserts in this volume, which have been created and tested in the Time-Life Books kitchens, are intended to successfully round out a meal. With moderation and balance as a guide in menu planning, you can always find a place for dessert at the table—especially if you prepare the desserts as directed here and serve them in the portions recommended, which average 175 calories. Indeed, nutritionists acknowledge that refined sugar in modest quantities is not harmful to a normal person's health though its sweetness tempts us to increase intake.

The recipes in this book strive to limit sugar, honey and other sweeteners to no more than two tablespoons per serving. (In some instances, such as among the frozen desserts, more sugar is needed to guarantee the proper end result.) Of course, sugar is not the sole caloric ingredient in a dessert. Surprisingly, a teaspoon of sugar contains only 16 calories. Fats such as butter, with about 33 calories per teaspoonful, weigh in at double that amount.

The fats in desserts—usually in the form of butter, cream or egg yolks—have traditionally made pie crusts flaky, mousses smooth, custards rich. All are of animal origin, however, and all contain saturated fats, which trigger a rise in the level of blood choles-terol, so strongly implicated in heart disease. But as the following recipes demonstrate, fats can be curbed without marring a dessert's appeal. Thus but-ter, cream and egg yolks appear in many of the reci-pes, but in moderate amounts—enough, certainly, to lend flavour or texture or both. Butter is generally lim-ited to half a tablespoon (7 g) per serving; sometimes it is paired with polyunsaturated margarine to achieve flakiness in pastry without increasing saturated fat. Cream is by and large restricted to a tablespoon per portion, and a single egg yolk is divided among four servings.

Throughout this book, the emphasis is on fresh, natural ingredients bursting with good flavour. There are no artificial sweeteners, no non-dairy creamers, no imitation egg yolks. Nor is carob substituted for chocolate; though carob has a somewhat similar ap-pearance and lacks saturated fat, its taste is very dif-ferent. Unsweetened cocoa powder, produced by ex-tracting fat from chocolate liquor, is used wherever it will not diminish texture and flavour. Oatmeal and nuts, strewn over a dessert as a garnish, provide pro-tein, vitamins, minerals such as iron and phosphorus, and fibre—the carbohydrate that is believed to pro-tect against cardiovascular disease and colon cancer. Whole-grain flours come into play, along with the more familiar white flours.

Flavour, not nutritional content, provides the incen-tive for including sweeteners in a dish. No sugar or syrup contains a significant amount of any nutrient. Honey, in particular, enjoys an undeserved reputation as a good source of minerals and B vitamins. How-ever, all honeys share an attribute that makes them a valued ingredient in cakes, biscuits and pastries: they are hygroscopic, meaning they absorb water. A des-sert baked with honey loses moisture more slowly and stays fresh longer than one made with another sweetener. On humid days, the honey may actually absorb moisture from the air.

The magic of fruit

Most of the desserts in this volume derive their spe-cial identity from fruit. The first of the book's five sec-tions is given over exclusively to recipes that feature fruit, but you will find fruit as well in the four other sections on frozen desserts, airy and creamy des-serts, dessert cakes and assemblies, and microwave cookery.

Fruit has many qualities to recommend it as a des-sert base. It is, to begin with, inherently sweet. Natu-ral sugar accounts for 20 per cent of the weight of a banana, and more than 60 per cent of the weight of a fresh date. For most fruits, the figure falls in the range of 10 to 15 per cent. (One food chemist has specu-lated that the word "lemon" has come to mean something unexpectedly faulty because it is a mouth-puckering aberration in its class, with a sugar content of only 1 per cent.) Despite their sweetness, most fruits are low in calories: weight for weight, they con-tain only one fifth the calories of sugars and syrups. Using fruits is an ideal way to create desserts that sat-isfy the calorie limit this book seeks to maintain for in-dividual servings.

Besides sweetness at a modest calorie count, fruits boast other advantages. They are good sources of fibre and, as a group, offer a whole alphabet of vita-mins. Potassium and phosphorus are among the min-erals that fruits contain, and they are remarkably low in sodium and fat. All of this nutritional bounty is wrapped up in packages of gorgeous colours and sculptured shapes, from the pale green contours of the honeydew melon to the shiny quilted oval of the blackberry.

There are many different varieties of fruits available in the shops. No matter what the season, there should be several types available at their peak of ma-turity: strawberries in the spring, raspberries, peaches and cherries in the summer, apples in the autumn, and oranges, lemons and grapefruit in the winter.

If you purchase fully ripe fruits, plan to use them within a day or two of their peak, for a decline in qual-ity soon sets in. (This is especially true of berries and grapes.) Most ripe fruits— including tropical ones—should be stored in the refrigerator to retard the shift into overripeness.

When only partially ripened fruit is available, keep it at room temperature out of direct sunlight. To speed the ripening process, pack the fruit loosely in a brown paper bag, then set the bag in a cool, dry spot and fold it closed. Check the contents of the bag every day and transfer the fruits to the refrigerator as they ripen. Containers made of glass, plastic or stainless steel are best for storage—some metals can impart an un-pleasant taste. Wash the fruit or wipe it clean with a damp cloth just before serving or preparing it.

The final flourish

Whatever dessert you prepare and whatever the oc-casion, presenting it attractively makes the eagerly awaited finale of a meal even sweeter. You may want to unmould a bombe on to a platter for all to admire before slicing it into serving portions. Glass dishes show off the radiant colours of fruits or sorbets, while small bowls or plates create the pleasant optical illusion that a diner's portion is larger than it is. In serving a well-chosen dessert in the style it deserves, you will have fulfilled its timeless role, bringing the meal to a happy and most satisfying conclusion.

The Key to Better Eating

Home Cooking addresses the concerns of today's weight-conscious, health-minded cooks with recipes that take into account guidelines set by nutritionists. The secret of eating well, of course, has to do with maintaining a balance of foods in the diet. The recipes thus should be used thoughtfully, in the context of a day's eating. To make the choice easier, an analysis is given of nutrients in a single serving. The counts for calories, protein, cholesterol, total fat, saturated fat and sodium are approximate.

Interpreting the chart

The chart below gives dietary guidelines for healthy men, women and children. Recommended figures vary from country to country, but the principles are the same everywhere. Here, the average daily amounts of calories and protein are from a report by the UK Department of Health and Social Security; the maximum advisable daily intake of fat is based on guidelines given by the National Advisory Committee on Nutrition Education (NACNE); those for cholesterol and sodium are based on upper limits suggested by the World Health Organization.

The volumes in the Home Cooking series do not purport to be diet books, nor do they focus on health foods. Rather, they express a common-sense approach to cooking that uses salt, sugar, cream, butter and oil in moderation while employing other ingredients that also provide flavour and satisfaction. The portions themselves are modest in size.

The recipes make few unusual demands. Naturally they call for fresh ingredients, offering substitutes when these are unavailable. (The substitute is not calculated in the nutrient analysis, however.)

Most of the ingredients can be found in any well-stocked supermarket.

Heavy-bottomed pots and pans are recommended to guard against burning whenever a small amount of oil is used and where there is danger of the food adhering to the hot surface, but non-stick pans can be utilized as well. Both safflower oil and virgin olive oil are favoured for sautéing. Safflower oil was chosen because it is the most highly polyunsaturated vegetable fat available in supermarkets, and polyunsaturated fats reduce blood cholesterol; if unobtainable, use sunflower oil, also high in polyunsaturated fats. Virgin olive oil is used because it has a fine fruity flavour lacking in the lesser grade known as "pure". In addition, it is—like all olive oil—high in mono-unsaturated fats, which are thought not to increase blood cholesterol. When virgin olive oil is unavailable, or when its flavour is not essential to the success of the dish, 'pure' may be used.

About cooking times

To help planning, time is taken into account in the recipes. While recognizing that everyone cooks at a different speed and that stoves and ovens differ, approximate "working" and "total" times are provided. Working time stands for the minutes actively spent on preparation; total time includes unattended cooking time, as well as time devoted to marinating, steeping or soaking ingredients. Since the recipes emphasize fresh foods, they may take a bit longer to prepare than 'quick and easy' dishes that call for canned or packaged products, but the difference in flavour, and often in nutrition, should compensate for the little extra time involved.

Recommended Dietary Guidelines

Average Daily Intake			Maximum Daily Intake			
	Calories	Protein grams	Cholesterol milligrams	Total fat grams	Saturated fat grams	Sodium milligrams
Females 7-8	1900	47	300	80	32	2000*
9-11	2050	51	300	77	35	2000
12-17	2150	53	300	81	36	2000
18-54	2150	54	300	81	36	2000
55-74	1900	47	300	72	32	2000
Males 7-8	1980	49	300	80	33	2000
9-11	2280	57	300	77	38	2000
12-14	2640	66	300	99	44	2000
15-17	2880	72	300	108	48	2000
18-34	2900	72	300	109	48	2000
35-64	2750	69	300	104	35	2000
65-74	2400	60	300	91	40	2000
						* (or 5g salt)

Amaretti

SERVE THESE ALMOND BISCUITS AS AN ACCOMPANIMENT TO CREAMY
DESSERTS AND SORBETS, OR ON THEIR OWN WITH YOUR FAVOURITE
AFTER-DINNER BEVERAGE.

Makes about 100 biscuits
Working time: about 30 minutes
Total time: about 9 hours (includes standing time)
Per biscuit: Calories 20, Protein 0g, Cholesterol 0mg, Total
fat 1g, Saturated fat 0g, Sodium 9mg

250 g/8 oz	*almond paste*
2 tsp	*pure almond extract*
200 g/7 oz	*caster sugar*
1/8 tsp	*salt*
	icing sugar

Mix together the almond paste, almond extract and
135 g (4 1/2 oz) of the sugar in a bowl. Beating continuously, gradually add about half of the egg whites.
Continue beating until the mixture has lightened in
texture and colour—about 3 minutes.

To prepare the meringue, beat the remaining egg
whites in a bowl until they are foamy. Add the salt,
then continue beating the whites until they form soft
peaks. Gradually add the remaining sugar, beating all
the while, until the whites form stiff peaks.

Fold one third of the meringue into the almond mixture to lighten it, then fold in the remaining meringue.
Spoon the mixture into a piping bag fitted with a plain
nozzle. Line two baking sheets with non-stick parchment paper and pipe out the mixture in mounds about
2.5 cm (1 inch) across. Sprinkle the mounds gener-
ously with icing sugar and let them stand at room
temperature for at least 8 hours.

Preheat the oven to 180°C (350°F or Mark 4).

To allow the amaretti to puff during baking, pinch a
mound at its base, cracking the surface. Pinch the
mound once more to crack its surface a second time
at a right angle to the first. Repeat the process to
crack all the amaretti.

Bake the amaretti, with the oven door propped
slightly ajar with the handle of a wooden spoon, for
30 minutes. Remove the biscuits from the oven and
let them stand, still on the paper, until they have
cooled to room temperature. Remove the amaretti
from the parchment paper, and store them in an airtight container until serving time.

*EDITOR'S NOTE: The almond paste called for in this
recipe is available in supermarkets.*

Amaretto Custards with Plum Sauce

Serves 6

Working time: about 30 minutes

Total time: about 1 hour and 30 minutes

Calories 250, Protein 8g, Cholesterol 100mg, Total fat 7g, Saturated fat 2g, Sodium 95mg

25 g/³/₄ oz	almonds, sliced
1¹/₄ tsp	ground cinnamon
5 tbsp	caster sugar
2	eggs, plus 2 egg whites
4 tbsp	amaretto liqueur
90 g/3 oz	honey
55 cl/18 fl oz	semi-skimmed milk
4	ripe red plums, quartered and stoned
2 tsp	fresh lemon juice

Preheat the oven to 170°C (325°F or Mark 3). Spread the almonds in a small baking tin and toast them in the oven as it preheats until they are golden—about 25 minutes.

Lightly butter six 12.5 cl (4 fl oz) ramekins, or other individual ovenproof moulds. In a small dish, mix ³/₄ teaspoon of the cinnamon with 2 tablespoons of the sugar. Put about 1 teaspoon of the cinnamon and-sugar mixture into each ramekin or mould, then tilt it in all directions to coat its buttered sides and bottom. Put the ramekins into a large, ovenproof baking dish and refrigerate them.

In a large bowl, whisk together the eggs, egg whites, amaretto, honey and the remaining ¹/₂ teaspoon of cinnamon. Whisk in the milk, then pour the mixture into the chilled ramekins, filling each to within 5 mm (¹/₄ inch) of the top.

Place the baking dish with the filled ramekins in the preheated oven. Pour enough hot tap water into the baking dish to come two thirds of the way up the sides of the ramekins. Bake the custards until a thin-bladed knife inserted in the centre of one comes out clean— about 30 minutes. Remove the ramekins from their water bath and let them stand for half an hour.

While the custards cool, prepare the plum sauce. Combine the plums, the remaining 3 tablespoons of sugar and the lemon juice in a food processor or a blender. Process the plums to a smooth purée, then pass the purée through a fine sieve into a bowl to remove the skins. Refrigerate the sauce until it is chilled— about half an hour.

To unmould the cooled custards, run a small, sharp knife round the inside of each ramekin. Invert a serving plate over the top and turn both over together. Lift away the ramekin; the custard should slip out easily. If it does not, rock the ramekin from side to side to loosen it. Ladle some of the plum sauce round each custard; sprinkle the toasted almonds over the top.

Apple Gateau

Serves 8

Working time: about 40 minutes

Total time: about 4 hours (includes chilling)

Calories 200, Protein 4g, Cholesterol 5mg, Total fat 2g, Saturated fat 0g, Sodium 180mg

1 kg/2¹/₂ lb	*cooking apples, peeled, cored and sliced*
90 g/3 oz	*granulated sugar*
2	*lemons, rind finely grated, juice of 1 strained*
250 g/8 oz	*breadcrumbs*
2 tsp	*freshly ground cinnamon*
90 g/3 oz	*demerara sugar*
2 tsp	*icing sugar*
1	*small red apple, cored, halved, cut into thin slices and brushed with lemon juice to prevent discolouration*
150 g/5 oz	*thick Greek yoghurt*

Put the cooking apples, granulated sugar, half the grated lemon rind and the lemon juice in a large saucepan. Cover with a tightly fitting lid and cook over a gentle heat until the apples are soft and fluffy. Pour the cooked apples into a large nylon sieve, and place the sieve over a bowl, to drain and cool.

Meanwhile, heat the oven to 200°C (400°F or Mark 6). Mix the breadcrumbs with the cinnamon and demerara sugar; spread the crumbs out in a thin layer on a large baking sheet. Brown them in the oven for about 20 minutes, stirring frequently with a fork to prevent the crumbs sticking together.

Reduce the heat to 180°C (350°F or Mark 4). Lightly oil a 20 cm (8 inch) springform tin, or loose-based cake tin; line the base with a round of non-stick parchment paper. Spread one third of the crumbs in the bottom of the tin, then spread half of the cooked apples evenly over the crumbs. Add half the remaining crumbs and then the remaining apples. Sprinkle the rest of the crumbs evenly over the top, pressing them down lightly. Bake for 35 minutes. Remove from the oven allow to cool, then refrigerate until cold.

Carefully transfer the gateau from the tin to a serving plate. Sift 1 teaspoon of the icing sugar over the top, and decorate with the red apple slices. Mix the yoghurt with the remaining icing sugar and lemon rind, and serve in a separate dish.

Apple-Filled Buckwheat Crêpes with Apple Syrup

Serves 4

Working time: about 1 hour

Total time: about 1 hour and 30 minutes

Calories 320, Protein 4g, Cholesterol 70mg, Total fat 11g, Saturated fat 2g, Sodium 95mg

1/2 litre/16 fl oz	*unsweetened apple juice*
500 g/1 lb	*sweet apples*
1/4 tsp	*ground cinnamon*
2 tbsp	*soured cream*
	crêpe batter
25 g/3/4 oz	*buckwheat flour*
75 g/21/2 oz	*plain flour*
1/8 tsp	*salt*
1	*egg*
2 tbsp	*plus 1/4 tsp safflower oil*

To prepare the crêpe batter, sift together the buckwheat flour, plain flour and salt In a large bowl, whisk together the egg, 2 tablespoons of the oil and 4 tablespoons of water. Gradually whisk in the sifted ingredients until a smooth mixture results. Cover the bowl and refrigerate the batter for at least 1 hour.

Bring 35 cl (12 fl oz) of the apple juice to the boil in a heavy-bottomed saucepan Lower the heat to medium low and boil the juice until it is reduced to 4 tablespoons—20 to 30 minutes Set the apple syrup aside

Peel, quarter and core the apples, then cut the quarters into 1 cm (1/2 inch) pieces. Combine the apple pieces with the cinnamon and the remaining apple juice in a large, shallow, heavy-bottomed pan set over medium heat. Cook the apple mixture, stirring occasionally, until almost all of the liquid has evaporated—15 to 20 minutes. Transfer the apple mixture to a food processor or a blender, and purée it. Return the purée to the pan and keep it in a warm place.

When the batter is chilled, heat a crêpe pan or a 20 cm (8 inch) frying pan over medium-high heat. Pour in the remaining 1/4 teaspoon of oil; with a paper towel, wipe the oil over the pan's entire cooking surface. Pour 2 to 3 tablespoons of the crêpe batter into the hot pan and immediately swirl the pan to coat the bottom with a thin, even layer of batter. Pour any excess batter back into the bowl. Cook the crêpe until the bottom is browned—about 21/2 minutes—then lift the edge with a spatula and turn the crêpe over. Cook the crêpe on the second side until it too is browned—15 to 30 seconds—and slide the crêpe on to a warmed plate. Repeat the process with the remaining batter to form eight crêpes in all.

Spread about 3 tablespoons of the warm apple purée over each crêpe. Fold each crêpe in half, then fold it in half again to produce a wedge shape Arrange two crêpes, one slightly overlapping the other, on each of four dessert plates Dribble a tablespoon of the apple syrup over each serving; garnish each dessert with 1/2 tablespoon of the soured cream and serve at once

Avocado and Grapefruit Bombe with Candied Rind

THIS ELEGANT PRESENTATION OF GRAPEFRUIT SORBET AND AVOCADO ICE MILK MAKES AN ELABORATE BUT PERFECT ENDING TO A SPECIAL MEAL.

Serves 12
Working time: about 1 hour
Total time: 2 to 4 hours, depending on freezing method
Calories 265, Protein 3g, Cholesterol 4mg, Total fat 9g, Saturated fat 2g, Sodium 30mg

Grapefruit sorbet
4 *large grapefruits*
300 g/10 oz *caster sugar*
Avocado ice milk
2 *large ripe avocados*
¹/₄ litre/8 fl oz *whole milk*
¹/₄ litre/8 fl oz *semi-skimmed milk*
100 g/3¹/₂ oz *caster sugar*
2 tbsp *finely chopped crystallized ginger*

Put a 1.5 litre (2¹/₂ pint) round mould into the freeze Using a vegetable peeler or a paring knife, pare the rind from two of the grapefruits. Cook the rind in a saucepan of boiling water for 10 minutes, then drain it. Julienne half of the rind and crystallize it. Set the candied rind aside. Put the uncandied rind into a food processor or a blender.

Remove the pith from the two pared grapefruits and discard it. Cut away all of the peel from the remaining two grapefruits and discard it too. Working over a bowl to catch the juice, cut between the membranes of the grapefruits to free the segments. Discard the seeds. Transfer the juice and the segments to the food processor or blender, and purée them with the uncandied rind. Add the sugar and process until it is dissolved. Freeze the grapefruit sorbet.

Remove the mould from the freezer and line it evenly with the sorbet, leaving a large hollow in the centre for the avocado mixture. Return the mould to the freezer.

Peel and stone the avocados, and purée their flesh. Blend in the whole milk, semi-skimmed milk and sugar. Freeze. Mix in the ginger half way through the freezing process.

When the ice milk is frozen, spoon it into the hollow in the grapefruit sorbet. Then freeze the mould for 1¹/₂ hours. Before serving, dip the bottom of the mould in hot water, then invert a chilled platter over the top and turn the two over together. Lift the mould away. Garnish the bombe with the candied grapefruit rind, and serve immediately.

Candied Citrus Rind

Makes about 60 g (2 oz)
Working time: about 20 minutes
Total time: about 35 minutes
Per tablespoon: Calories 16, Protein 0g, Cholesterol 0mg, Total fat 0g, Saturated fat 0g, Sodium 0mg

45 g/1¹/₂ oz *julienned citrus rind (orange, grapefruit, lemon or lime)*
4 tbsp *caster sugar*

Put the citrus rind into a saucepan with ¹/₄ litre (8 fl oz) of water and bring the water to the boil. Cook the rind for 15 minutes, then remove it with a slotted spoon, and spread it on paper towels to drain. Pour the water out of the saucepan. Add the sugar, 2 tablespoons of cold water and the drained rind to the pan. Cook the mixture over high heat, stirring constantly, until the rind is coated with white, crystallized sugar—about 3 minutes. Remove the rind from the pan and set it on greaseproof paper to dry.

EDITOR'S NOTE: Candied rind may be stored in an airtight container at room temperature for up to a week.

Baked Apples Filled with Cranberries and Sultanas

Serves 6

Working time: about 20 minutes

Total time: about 40 minutes

Calories 210, Protein 1g, Cholesterol 8mg, Total fat 4g, Saturated fat 2g, Sodium 8mg

250 g/8 oz *fresh or frozen cranberries*
90 g/3 oz *light brown sugar*
3 tbsp *sultanas, chopped*
25 g/³/₄ oz *unsalted butter*
6 *Golden Delicious apples*

Put the cranberries into a glass bowl and sprinkle the brown sugar over them. Cover the bowl with plastic film and microwave the berries on high for 2 minutes. Stir in the sultanas and 15 g (¹/₂ oz) of the butter, re-cover the bowl, and cook the mixture on high until the berries start to burst—1¹/₂ to 2¹/₂ minutes. Stir the mixture well and set it aside.

Core one of the apples with a melon baller or a small spoon, scooping out the centre of the apple to form a conical cavity about 3 cm (1¹/₄ inches) wide at the top and only 1 cm (¹/₂ inch) wide at the bottom. Using a cannelle knife or a paring knife, cut two grooves for decoration round the apple. Prepare the other apples the same way.

Fill the apples with the cranberry mixture. Arrange the apples in a ring round the edge of a glass pie plate and dot them with the remaining butter. Cover the filled apples with greaseproof paper and microwave them on high for 5 minutes. Rotate the plate and each apple 180 degrees, and microwave the apples on high for 3 to 5 minutes more. Let the apples stand for about 5 minutes before serving them with their baking juices ladled over the top.

Baked Chocolate Custards

Serves 8
Working time: about 30 minutes
Total time: about 2 hours

Calories 110, Protein 4g, Cholesterol 75mg, Total fat 3g,
Saturated fat 1g, Sodium 70mg

2 *eggs*
100 g/3¹/₂ oz *caster sugar*
2 tbsp *unsweetened cocoa powder*
¹/₁₆ tsp *salt*
¹/₂ litre/16 fl oz *semi-skimmed milk*
45 g/1¹/₂ oz *fresh raspberries (optional)*

Preheat the oven to 170°C (325°F or Mark 3). Whisk together the eggs, sugar, cocoa powder and salt in a heatproof bowl. Heat the milk in a small saucepan just until it comes to the boil. Whisking continuously, pour the hot milk into the bowl. Thoroughly mix in the milk, then pour the mixture into the saucepan.

Cook the mixture over low heat, stirring constantly with a wooden spoon, until it has thickened enough to lightly coat the back of the spoon. Strain the mixture into eight individual ovenproof custard cups or ramekins. Set the custard cups in a roasting pan or casserole with sides at least 1 cm (¹/₂ inch) higher than the cups. Pour enough boiling water into the pan to come half way up the sides of the cups. Cover the pan with a baking sheet or a piece of aluminium foil, then put it in the oven, and bake the custards until the centre of one barely quivers when the cup is shaken—20 to 30 minutes.

Remove the pan from the oven and uncover it. Leave the custard cups in the water until they cool to room temperature, then refrigerate them for at least 30 minutes. If you like, arrange several fresh raspberries on each custard before serving them.

Banana Crème Caramel

Serves 8

Working time: about 45 minutes

Total time: about 3 hours and 15 minutes

Calories 160, Protein 3g, Cholesterol 70mg, Total fat 2g,
Saturated fat 1g, Sodium 35mg

165 g/5½ oz *sugar*
4 tsp *fresh lemon juice*
¼ litre/8 fl oz *semi-skimmed milk*
2 *eggs*
1 tbsp *dark rum*
1 tsp *pure vanilla extract*
¼ tsp *ground cardamom or cinnamon*
¼ litre/8 fl oz *puréed banana (from 2 to 3 bananas)*
2 *bananas, peeled and diagonally sliced*

Preheat the oven to 170°C (325°F or Mark 3).

Begin by caramelizing a 1 litre (2 pint) souffle dish or a 15 cm (6 inch) diameter cake tin. In a small heavybottomed saucepan, combine 100 g (3½ oz) of the sugar, 1 teaspoon of the lemon juice and 3 tablespoons of water. Cook the mixture over medium-high heat until the syrup caramelizes—it will have a rich brown hue. Immediately remove the saucepan from the heat. Working quickly, pour the caramel into the souffle dish or cake tin. Using oven gloves to protect your hands, tilt the dish in all directions to coat the bottom and about 2.5 cm (1 inch) of the adjacent sides. Continue tilting the dish until the caramel has hardened, then set the dish aside.

To prepare the custard, put the milk into a heavy-bottomed saucepan over medium heat. As soon as the milk reaches the boil, remove the pan from the heat and set it aside. In a bowl, whisk together the eggs and the remaining sugar, then stir in the rum, vanilla extract, cardamom or cinnamon, puréed banana, and the remaining 3 teaspoons of lemon juice. Stirring constantly to avoid curdling the eggs, pour the hot milk into the banana mixture. Transfer the custard to the caramelized dish.

Set the custard dish in a small roasting pan and pour enough hot tap water into the pan to come 2.5 cm (1 inch) up the sides of the custard dish. Bake the custard until a knife inserted in the centre comes out clean— 20 to 30 minutes. (Take care not to insert the knife so deep that it pierces the caramel coating.) Remove the custard from the hot-water bath and let it cool to room temperature. Put the custard into the refrigerator until it is chilled—about 2 hours.

To unmould, invert a serving plate over the top of the dish, then turn both over together. The dish should lift away easily; if not, turn the dish right side up again and run a small, sharp knife round the top of the custard to loosen it. Garnish with a ring of banana slices. Cut the custard into wedges and spoon some of the caramel sauce over each one before serving.

Blackberry Timbales
with Almond Cream

Serves 8

Working time: about 45 minutes

Total time: about 2 hours and 45 minutes (includes chilling)

Calories 280, Protein 9g, Cholesterol 30mg, Total fat 8g, Saturated fat 5g, Sodium 170mg

---

5 tsp *powdered gelatine*
300 g/10 oz *blackberries*
135 g/4¹/₂ oz *caster sugar*
¹/₄ tsp *salt*
¹/₂ litre/16 fl oz   *plain low-fat yoghurt*
4 tbsp *fresh lime juice*
6 tbsp *amaretto liqueur*
Almond cream
35 cl/12 fl oz *semi-skimmed milk*
4 *egg whites*
12.5 cl/4 fl oz *double cream*
4 tbsp *caster sugar*
¹/₂ tsp *pure vanilla extract*
¹/₈ tsp *almond extract*
2 tbsp *amaretto liqueur*
2 *limes, thinly sliced, for garnish*

To prepare the timbales, sprinkle the gelatine over 4 tablespoons of water in a cup and let it soften for 5 minutes. Purée all but eight of the blackberries in a food processor or a blender. Strain the purée into a heavy-bottomed non-reactive saucepan. Stir the sugar, salt and softened gelatine into the purée. Warm the purée over low heat, stirring occasionally, until the gelatine and sugar dissolve—2 to 3 minutes. Transfer the purée to a bowl.

In another bowl, whisk together the yoghurt, lime juice and amaretto. Pour this mixture into the blackberry purée, whisking constantly. Tap the bottom of the bowl on the work surface to collapse any large air bubbles, then spoon the mixture into eight fluted timbale moulds or individual jelly moulds. Refrigerate the timbales until they have set—about 2 hours.

While the timbales are chilling, prepare the almond cream. Bring ¹/₄ litre (8 fl oz) of the milk to the boil in a clean heavy-bottomed saucepan, then immediately remove the pan from the heat. Whisk the egg whites in a clean bowl until they are frothy. Add the cream, the sugar and the remaining unheated milk. Whisking constantly, slowly pour the hot milk into the egg white mixture in a thin, steady stream; pouring slowly keeps the egg whites from forming clumps.

Return the mixture to the saucepan in which you heated the milk. Stirring constantly, thicken the sauce over medium heat until it coats the back of the spoon—4 to 5 minutes. Remove the saucepan from the heat; stir in the vanilla and almond extracts and amaretto. Transfer the sauce to a bowl. Lay a sheet of plastic film directly on the surface of the sauce to prevent its forming a skin, and put the sauce into the refrigerator until it is chilled—about 2 hours.

To unmould a timbale, briefly dip the bottom of the mould in warm water. Invert a dessert plate over the mould, then turn the two over together, and lift away the mould. Repeat the process to unmould the other timbales. Spoon some of the sauce round each timbale and garnish each plate with a slice of lime and one of the reserved blackberries.

Bananas and Oranges in Chocolate Puffs

Serves 16
Working time: about 45 minutes
Total time: about 1 hour and 45 minutes

Calories 160, Protein 5g, Cholesterol 60mg, Total fat 6g, Saturated fat 2g, Sodium 70mg

150 g/5 oz	*plain flour*
1 tbsp	*unsweetened cocoa powder*
1 tsp	*ground cinnamon*
¹/₂ tsp	*grated nutmeg*
30 g/1 oz	*unsalted butter*
2 tbsp	*safflower oil*
¹/₄ tsp	*salt*
2 tbsp	*caster sugar*
3	*eggs, plus 2 egg whites*
4	*ripe bananas*
4	*oranges, segmented*

Ricotta filling

225 g/7¹/₂ oz	*low-fat ricotta cheese*
2 tbsp	*caster sugar*
1 tsp	*pure vanilla extract*
2 tbsp	*icing sugar*

Mix together the flour, cocoa powder, cinnamon and nutmeg; set the mixture aside. Preheat the oven to 200°C (400°F or Mark 6).

Combine the butter, oil, salt, sugar and ¹/₄ litre (8 fl oz) of water in a saucepan, and bring the mixture to the boil. As soon as the butter melts, remove the pan from the heat and stir in the flour mixture with a wooden spoon. Return the pan to the stove over medium heat and cook the mixture, stirring vigorously, until it comes cleanly away from the sides of the pan.

Remove the pan from the heat once more and allow it to cool for 2 minutes before adding the eggs. Incorporate the whole eggs one at a time, beating vigorously after you add each one, until the dough is smooth. In a separate bowl, whisk the egg whites until they are frothy; beat half of the egg whites into the dough. To test the consistency of the dough, scoop some up with a spoon, then turn the spoon and wait for the dough to fall off; it should fall off cleanly at the count of three. If it does not, beat in more of the egg whites and repeat the test.

Spoon the dough into a piping bag fitted with a 1 cm (¹/₂ inch) star nozzle. Pipe the dough on to a lightly oiled baking sheet in mounting swirls about 4 cm (1¹/₂ inches) across. (If you do not have a piping bag, fashion 4 cm/1¹/₂ inch mounds with a spoon.) Bake the puffs until they expand and are firm to the touch— about 25 minutes. Turn off the oven, prop the door ajar with a wooden spoon, and let the puffs dry in the

oven for 15 minutes. Then transfer them to a rack to cool.

While the puffs are cooling, make the filling: purée the ricotta in a food processor or a blender, then blend in the sugar and vanilla. Refrigerate the filling.

To assemble the dessert, cut each puff in half horizontally. Fill the lower halves with the chilled ricotta mixture. Peel the bananas and slice them into rounds; then arrange the banana rounds and orange segments on top of the filling. Replace the upper halves of the puffs. Sift the icing sugar over all, and serve the puffs at once.

Berry-Filled Meringue Baskets

Serves 8
Working time: about 50 minutes
Total time: about 5 hours (includes drying)
Calories 150, Protein 4g, Cholesterol 5mg, Total fat 2g,
Saturated fat 1g, Sodium 45mg

200 g/7 oz *caster sugar*
125 g/4 oz *low-fat ricotta cheese*
4 tbsp *plain low-fat yoghurt*
350 g/12 oz *hulled, sliced strawberries*
150 g/5 oz *blueberries, stemmed, picked over and rinsed*

Line a baking sheet with non-stick parchment paper or brown paper. Preheat the oven to 70°C (160°F or Mark 1/4). If your oven does not have a setting this low, set it at its lowest. Keep the oven door propped open with a ball of crumpled foil.

To prepare the meringue, put the egg whites and sugar into a large, heatproof bowl. Set the bowl over a pan of simmering water, and stir the mixture with a whisk until the sugar has dissolved and the egg whites are hot—about 6 minutes. Remove the bowl from the heat. Using an electric mixer, beat the egg whites on medium-high speed until they form stiff peaks and have cooled to room temperature.

Transfer the meringue to a piping bag fitted with a 1 cm (1/2 inch) nozzle. Holding the nozzle about 1 cm (1/2 inch) above the surface of the baking sheet, pipe out the meringue in a tightly coiled spiral until you have formed a flat disc about 8.5 cm (3 1/2 inches) across. Pipe a single ring of meringue on top of the edge of the disc, forming a low wall that will hold in the filling. Form seven more meringue baskets in the same way.

Put the baking sheet into the oven and let the meringues bake for at least 4 hours. The meringues should remain white and be thoroughly dried out. Let meringues stand at room temperature until cool—they will become quite crisp.

Purée the ricotta with the yoghurt in a food processor or a blender. Divide the cheese mixture among meringue baskets, and top each with some of strawberries and blueberries

Cherry Ice Cream

Serves 8

Working time: about 30 minutes

Total time: 1 to 3 hours, depending on freezing method

Calories 180, Protein 8g, Cholesterol 16mg, Total fat 6g,
Saturated fat 3g, Sodium 90mg

350 g/12 oz *sweet cherries*
100 g/3 oz *sugar*
350 g/12 oz *low-fat ricotta cheese*
12.5 cl/4 fl oz *plain low-fat yoghurt*
$^1/_2$ tsp *almond extract*
$^1/_2$ tsp *pure vanilla extract*
12.5 cl/4 fl oz *semi-skimmed milk*
2 tbsp *toasted almonds, crushed*
2 *egg whites*

Stone and quarter the cherries, working over a large
bowl to catch any juice. Put the stoned cherries, the
sugar and 12.5 cl (4 fl oz) of water in a heavy-bottomed saucepan. Bring the liquid to the boil over medium-high heat, then reduce the heat and simmer the
cherries for 10 minutes.

Remove the cherries from the syrup with a slotted
spoon and continue cooking the syrup until it is reduced by one half—about 5 minutes. Refrigerate the
cherries and half of the syrup.

Put the ricotta, yoghurt, almond extract and vanilla
extract into a food processor or a blender. Purée the
mixture, stopping at least once to scrape down the
sides, until you have a very smooth purée. Stir the
cherries and the syrup into the ricotta mixture, then
add the milk, almonds and egg whites, and mix well.
Freeze the mixture. If you are using the food processor method, do not add the cherries and almonds until after you have processed the mixture.

Cherry Puffs

Serves 12

Working time: about 1 hour and 10 minutes

Total time: about 2 hours

Calories 170, Protein 5g, Cholesterol 75mg, Total fat 7g, Saturated fat 2g, Sodium 80mg

750 g/1¹/₂ lb	*sweet cherries, stoned*	
4	*lemons, grated rind only*	
12.5 cl/4 fl oz	*fresh lemon juice*	
2 tbsp	*cornflour*	
4 tbsp	*kirsch*	
17.5 cl/6 fl oz	*plain low-fat yoghurt*	
2 tbsp	*caster sugar*	

Choux paste

30 g/1 oz	*unsalted butter*
2 tbsp	*safflower oil*
¹/₄ tsp	*salt*
1 tsp	*caster sugar*
150 g/5 oz	*plain flour*
3	*eggs, plus 2 egg whites*

Combine the cherries, lemon rind and lemon juice in a saucepan over medium-high heat. Bring the mixture to the boil, then reduce the heat to maintain a simmer, and cook the mixture for 5 minutes. Combine the cornflour with the kirsch in a small bowl and stir them into the cherry mixture. Continue cooking, stirring constantly, until the mixture thickens—about 2 minutes. Set the cherry filling aside at room temperature.

Whisk together the yoghurt and sugar in a small bowl; refrigerate the bowl.

Preheat the oven to 220°C (425°F or Mark 7).

To make the choux paste, combine the butter, oil, salt, sugar and ¹/₄ litre (8 fl oz) of water in a heavy-bottomed saucepan. Bring the mixture to the boil over medium-high heat. As soon as the butter melts, remove the pan from the heat and stir in the flour with a wooden spoon. Return the pan to the stove over medium heat; cook the mixture, stirring constantly, until it comes cleanly away from the sides of the pan and leaves a slight film on the bottom.

Remove the pan from the heat once more and allow it to cool for 2 minutes before adding the eggs Incorporate the eggs one at a time, beating well after you add each one, until a smooth dough results. In a separate bowl, whisk the egg whites until they are frothy; beat one half of the egg whites into the dough. To test the consistency of the dough, scoop some up with a spoon, then turn the spoon and wait for the dough to fall off; it should fall off cleanly at the count of three. If it does not, beat more of the egg whites into the dough.

Spoon the dough into a piping bag fitted with a 1 cm (¹/₂ inch) plain nozzle. Pipe the dough on to a lightly oiled baking sheet in 12 mounting swirls about 5 cm (2 inches) in diameter and 5 cm (2 inches) apart. (If you do not have a piping bag, fashion the swirls with a spoon.) Bake the swirls until they puff up and are uniformly browned—about 25 minutes. Turn off the oven, prop the door ajar with the handle of a wooden spoon, and let the puffs dry in the oven for 15 minutes. Transfer the puffs to a rack to cool.

To assemble the puffs, slice each in half horizontally and spoon the cherry filling into the bottoms. Top each filling with a tablespoon of the sweetened yoghurt; replace the tops and serve the puffs immediately.

Chocolate Chiffon Cake with Raspberry Filling

Serves 12

Working time: about 40 minutes

Total time: about 2 hours

Calories 205, Protein 3g, Cholesterol 45mg, Total fat 6g, Saturated fat 1g, Sodium 110mg

4 tbsp *unsweetened cocoa powder*
100 g/3¹/₂ oz *plain flour*
150 g/5 oz *caster sugar*
1 tsp *bicarbonate of soda*
¹/₈ tsp *salt*
4 tbsp *safflower oil*
2 *eggs, separated, plus 2 egg whites, the whites at room temperature*
l tsp *pure vanilla extract*
¹/₄ tsp *cream of tartar*

Raspberry filling

250 g/8 oz *fresh or frozen raspberries*
100 g/3¹/₂ oz *sugar*

Raspberry-champagne sauce

250 g/8 oz *fresh or frozen raspberries, thawed*
¹/₂ tsp *fresh lemon juice*
17.5 cl/6 fl oz *chilled dry champagne (¹/₄-bottle)*
2 tbsp *caster sugar (if you are using fresh raspberries)*

Spoon the cocoa powder into a small heatproof bowl and stir in 12.5 cl (4 fl oz) of boiling water. Set the bowl aside. Preheat the oven to 180°C (350°F or Mark 4).

Sift the flour, half the caster sugar, the bicarbonate of soda and salt into a large bowl. Stir in the oil, egg yolks, the cocoa mixture and the vanilla; mix to blend the ingredients.

Pour the egg whites into a bowl and beat them until they are frothy. Add the cream of tartar, then continue beating the whites until soft peaks form. Gradually adding the remaining sugar, beat the whites until they form stiff peaks. Mix one third of the beaten whites into the flour mixture to lighten it; gently fold in the remaining whites. Pour the mixture into a 23 by 12.5 by 7.5 cm (9 by 5 by 3 inch) loaf tin. Bake the cake until a wooden toothpick inserted in the centre comes out clean—about 55 minutes. Invert the tin on a cake rack and let the cake cool completely.

While the cake is cooling, make the raspberry filling. Combine the raspberries, sugar and 2 tablespoons of water in a heavy saucepan over medium heat; cook the mixture, stirring constantly, until it has the consistency of jam—about 25 minutes. Refrigerate the filling.

For the sauce, purée the raspberries with the lemon juice in a food processor or a blender. (If you are using fresh raspberries, include the 2 tablespoons of sugar in the purée.) Strain the purée into a bowl; discard the solids. Refrigerate the purée.

Run a knife blade round the sides of the loaf tin, then invert the tin again and rap it sharply against the work surface to unmould the cake. Cut the cake into two horizontal layers. Spread the chilled raspberry filling over the bottom layer, then set the top layer back in place. Just before serving, stir the champagne into the chilled raspberry purée. Cut the cake into serving slices, and surround each one with a little of the raspberry-champagne sauce.

Chilled Lemon Mousse with Blueberries

Serves 8

Working time: about 35 minutes

Total time: about 1 hour and 30 minutes

Calories 215, Protein 3g, Cholesterol 50mg, Total fat 7g, Saturated fat 4g, Sodium 45mg

2	*lemons*
	1 *egg, plus 1 egg white*
225 g/7¹/₂ oz	*caster sugar*
60 g/2 oz	*unsalted butter, melted*
500 g/1 lb	*fresh blueberries, picked over and rinsed*
4	*egg whites*
¹/₈ tsp	*cream of tartar*

Grate the rind of the lemons and put it in the top of a double boiler. Squeeze the juice from the lemons and add it to the rind. Whisk the egg, egg white and 200 g (7 oz) of the sugar into the lemon mixture, and set it over simmering water. Cook the mixture, stirring continuously, until it thickens—12 to 15 minutes. (Do not overcook the mixture or it will curdle.)

Remove the double boiler from the heat and mix in the butter. Set the top of the double boiler in a larger bowl filled with ice and let the mixture cool, whisking it occasionally.

To prepare the meringue, put the egg whites and the cream of tartar into a bowl, and beat them until soft peaks form. Add a little of the remaining sugar and continue beating the egg whites, gradually adding the rest of the sugar, until stiff peaks have formed and the meringue is glossy.

Stir a few heaped spoonfuls of the meringue into the cooled lemon mixture to lighten it. Fold in the remaining meringue and all but 90 g (3 oz) of the blueberries. Spoon the lemon mousse into parfait glasses and chill for at least 1 hour before serving. Garnish each serving with a few of the reserved blueberries.

Raspberry Mousse

Serves 8

Working time: about 20 minutes

Total time: about 1 hour

Calories 150, Protein 4g, Cholesterol 25mg, Total fat 6g, Saturated fat 4g, Sodium 40mg

2¹/₂ tsp	*powdered gelatine*
100 g/3¹/₂ oz	*sugar*
400 g/14 oz	*fresh or frozen whole raspberries, thawed*
¹/₄ litre/8 fl oz	*plain low-fat yoghurt*
12.5 cl/4 fl oz	*double cream*
2	*egg whites*

Sprinkle the gelatine on to 4 tablespoons of water and let the gelatine soften while you prepare the raspberries. Set 24 berries aside to use as garnish. Pour 4 tablespoons of water into a saucepan; stir in the sugar and the remaining raspberries. Over medium heat, simmer the mixture for 4 minutes. Add the softened gelatine and stir until it dissolves—about 30 seconds.

Transfer the raspberry mixture to a blender or a food processor and purée it. Strain the purée through a fine sieve into a bowl. Refrigerate the purée until it is cool, then stir in the yoghurt.

Whip the cream until it forms stiff peaks. Fold the whipped cream into the raspberry mixture.

Beat the egg whites in a bowl until stiff peaks form when the beater is lifted from the bowl. Fold the egg whites into the raspberry mixture.

Fill each of eight wine glasses with the raspberry mousse. Chill the mousse for at least 30 minutes; just before serving, garnish each mousse with three of the reserved raspberries.

Crêpes with Glazed Pears

Serves 4

Working time: about 1 hour

Total time: about 3 hours

Calories 305, Protein 5g, Cholesterol 80mg, Total fat 11g, Saturated fat 3g, Sodium 70mg

3 ripe pears
1 tbsp fresh lemon juice
¹/₂ tsp safflower oil
4 tbsp Sauternes or other sweet white wine
3 tbsp honey
15 g/¹/₂ oz unsalted butter
freshly ground black pepper

Sauternes crêpe batter

7 tbsp plain flour
¹/₁₆ tsp salt
freshly ground black pepper
¹/₈ tsp caster sugar
1 egg
2 tbsp Sauternes or other sweet white wine
1¹/₂ tbsp safflower oil
12.5 to 17.5 cl/
4 to 6 fl oz semi-skimmed milk

To prepare the crêpe batter, whisk together the flour, salt, some pepper, the sugar, egg, wine, oil and 12.5 cl (4 fl oz) of the milk in a bowl. Whisking constantly, pour in enough additional milk in a fine, steady stream to thin the batter to the consistency of double cream. Cover the bowl and refrigerate it for at least 2 hours.

Peel, core and slice the pears. Sprinkle the slices with the lemon juice and set them aside while you cook the crêpes.

Heat a crêpe pan or a 20 cm (8 inch) non-stick frying pan over medium-high heat. Pour in the ¹/₂ teaspoon of oil and spread it over the entire surface with a paper towel. Pour 2 to 3 tablespoons of the batter into the hot pan and swirl the pan just enough to coat the bottom with a thin, even layer of batter. Pour any excess batter back into the bowl. Cook the crêpe until the bottom is brown—about 30 seconds—then lift the edge of the crêpe and turn it over. Cook the second side until it is brown—about 15 seconds more—and slide the crêpe on to a plate. The crêpe should be paper thin; if it is not, stir a little more milk into the batter. Repeat the process with the remaining batter to form eight crêpes in all. If you are using a crêpe pan, you may have to oil it again to prevent sticking.

Fold a crêpe in half, then in thirds. Repeat the process to fold the remaining crêpes. Put two on each of four dessert plates, and set them aside in a warm place.

Bring the wine and honey to the boil in a sauté or frying pan over medium-high heat. Cook the mixture until it is syrupy—about 2 minutes. Add the butter and the pears, and continue cooking until the pears are barely tender and have become glazed with the mixture—about 3 minutes more.

With a slotted spoon, remove the pears from the pan and divide them evenly among the four plates. Pour a little of the syrup remaining in the pan over each portion; grind a generous amount of black pepper over all and serve at once.

27

Frozen Nectarine and Plum Terrine

Serves 10
Working time: about 45 minutes
Total time: about 1 day (includes freezing)
Calories 190, Protein 1g, Cholesterol 0mg, Total fat 1g,
Saturated fat 0g, Sodium 1mg

Nectarine sorbet
500 g/1 lb *nectarines, halved and stoned*
12.5 cl/4 fl oz *fresh orange juice*
4 tbsp *fresh lemon juice*
150 g/5 oz *caster sugar*

Plum sorbet
500 g/1 lb *plums, halved and stoned*
17.5 cl/6 fl oz *fresh orange juice*
150 g/5 oz *caster sugar*

Garnish
1 *nectarine, halved, stoned and sliced into thin wedges*
2 *plums, halved, stoned and sliced into thin wedges*

To prepare the nectarine sorbet, purée the nectarines, orange juice, lemon juice and sugar in a food processor or blender. Transfer the purée to a freezer container and freeze it. Prepare the plum sorbet in the same way and freeze it as well.

When both sorbets are firm but not hard, line a 1.5 litre (2½ pint) loaf tin or metal mould with plastic film.

Put half the nectarine sorbet into the lined tin, smoothing it out with a rubber spatula. Top the nectarine sorbet with half of the plum sorbet; smooth its top the same way. Repeat the layering process with the remaining sorbet to make four layers in all. To collapse any air bubbles, tap the bottom of the tin on the work surface. Cover the top of the sorbet with plastic film and freeze the terrine overnight.

Remove the plastic film from the top. Invert the terrine on to a chilled platter. Unwrap the terrine and cut it into 1 cm (½ inch) slices, dipping the knife into hot water and wiping it off between slices. Garnish the slices with the wedges of nectarine and plum.

28

Fruit-and-Nut-Filled Phyllo Roll

Serves 6

Working time: about 40 minutes

Total time: about 1 hour and 10 minutes

Calories 185, Protein 4g, Cholesterol 8mg, Total fat 6g,
Saturated fat 2g, Sodium 2mg

1 *egg white*
60 g/2 oz *low-fat ricotta cheese*
1 *orange*
1 tsp *grated lemon rind*
$^1/_4$ tsp *ground cinnamon*
$^1/_8$ tsp *grated nutmeg*
$^1/_8$ tsp *ground all spice*
$^1/_8$ tsp *salt*
3 tbsp *coarsely chopped pecan nuts*
75 g/2$^1/_2$ oz *raisins*
1 tbsp *pure maple syrup*
4 tbsp *caster sugar*
2 *slices wholemeal bread, toasted*
2 *sheets frozen phyllo, thawed*
15 g/$^1/_2$ oz *unsalted butter, melted*

To make the filling, first mix together the egg white and the ricotta. With a vegetable peeler or a paring knife, remove the rind from the orange and reserve it. Cut away all the white pith and discard it. Working over a bowl to catch the juice, segment the orange, dropping the segments into the bowl. Squeeze the last drops of juice from the pulpy core of membranes into the bowl. Coarsely chop the orange rind and orange segments, and add them to the ricotta mixture along with the juice that has collected in the bowl. Stir in the lemon rind, cinnamon, nutmeg, allspice, salt, pecans, raisins, maple syrup and sugar. Cut the toasted bread slices into cubes and mix them into the filling. Set the filling aside.

Preheat the oven to 180°C (325°F or Mark 4).

Lay one of the phyllo sheets on a piece of greaseproof paper that is slightly larger than the phyllo. Lightly brush the phyllo with some of the butter. Set the second sheet of phyllo squarely on top of the first.

Spoon the filling down one of the longer sides of the double phyllo sheet, leaving about 4 cm (1$^1/_2$ inches) uncovered at both ends of the filling. To avoid tearing the phyllo, lift the edge of the greaseproof paper and roll the phyllo once round the filling. Continue rolling the phyllo and filling away from you to form a compact cylinder. Tuck under the two open ends of the roll and transfer it to a lightly oiled baking sheet. Brush the top of the roll with the remaining butter and bake it until it is golden-brown—about 30 minutes. Allow the roll to cool, then slice it into serving rounds.

Ginger-Date Ice Cream

THE CREAMY TEXTURE OF THIS LOW-FAT ICE CREAM COMES FROM THE
PAIRING OF RICOTTA CHEESE AND YOGHURT.

Serves 8
Working time: about 25 minutes
Total time: 1 to 3 hours, depending on freezing method
Calories 120, Protein 6g, Cholesterol 12mg, Total fat 3g,
Saturated fat 2g, Sodium 75mg

¹/₄ litre/8 fl oz *semi-skimmed milk*
   125 g/4 oz *dried stoned dates, cut into small pieces*
    6 tbsp *plain low-fat yoghurt*
  250 g/8 oz *low-fat ricotta cheese*
    2 tbsp *caster sugar*
    2 *egg whites*
    1 tbsp *finely chopped crystallized ginger*
  ¹/₂ tbsp *fresh lemon juice*

Warm the milk in a saucepan over very low heat. Remove the pan from the heat and add all but 2 tablespoons of the dates; steep the dates for 10 minutes.

Purée the date-milk mixture in a food processor or a blender, then transfer the purée to a large bowl.

Purée the yoghurt, ricotta cheese and sugar in the food processor or blender, stopping at least once to scrape down the sides, until you have a very smooth purée. Add the yoghurt-ricotta purée to the date-milk purée in the bowl, and whisk the two together. Refrigerate the bowl for 15 minutes.

Blend the egg whites into the refrigerated purée, then freeze the mixture. If you plan to use an ice cream maker, stir the crystallized ginger, lemon juice and reserved 2 tablespoons of dates into the mixture before freezing it. If you are using the hand-whisking method, stir in the lemon juice, ginger and reserved dates when the mixture is almost solid. For the food processor method, add the lemon juice during the processing, then blend in the ginger and reserved dates.

Greek Yoghurt Flan

Serves 8

Working time: about 40 minutes

Total time: about 3 hours (includes chilling)

Calories 115, Protein 3g, Cholesterol 60mg, Total fat 3g,
Saturated fat 1g, Sodium 40mg

2	*eggs*
1	*egg white*
90 g/3 oz	*caster sugar*
90 g/3 oz	*plain flour*
250 g/8 oz	*thick Greek yoghurt*
1 tbsp	*sifted icing sugar*
1	*orange, finely grated rind only*
3 tbsp	*orange juice mixed with 3 tbsp cointreau*
8	*fresh ripe figs, each cut into 8 pieces, skin removed if bitter*

Heat the oven to 180°C (350°F or Mark 4). Butter a 22 cm (10 inch) fluted sponge flan tin. Put the eggs, egg white and sugar into a large bowl and prepare the sponge mixture as shown below. Pour the mixture into the prepared tin and spread it evenly. Bake for 25 minutes, until very lightly browned and springy to the touch. Turn out on to a wire rack to cool.

Put one third of the yoghurt into a piping bag fitted with a star nozzle and refrigerate until needed. Mix the remaining yoghurt with the icing sugar and the finely grated orange rind.

Place the sponge flan on a serving dish. Spoon the orange juice and cointreau evenly over the centre of the flan, then spread the orange-flavoured yoghurt on top. Pipe a decorative border round the edge with the yoghurt in the piping bag. Arrange the fig pieces on the yoghurt in the centre. Cover loosely with plastic film and chill in the refrigerator for 1 hour before serving.

Honey-Glazed Buttermilk Cake

Serves 16
Working time: about 30 minutes
Total time: about 2 hours and 30 minutes
Calories 310, Protein 6g, Cholesterol 10mg, , Total fat 6g,
Saturated fat 3g, Sodium 190mg

375 g/13 oz *plain flour*
1 tsp *bicarbonate of soda*
450 g/15 oz *caster sugar*
60 g/2 oz *unsalted butter, cut into 1 cm (¹/₂ inch)*
pats
60 g/2 oz *polyunsaturated margarine*
2 tsp *pure vanilla extract*
35 cl/12 fl oz *buttermilk*
4 *egg whites*
1 *lemon, grated rind only*
Honey glaze
4 tbsp *sugar*
4 tbsp *butter milk*
90 g/3 oz *honey*
¹/₂ tsp *pure vanilla extract*

Grease a 3 litre (5 pint) kugelhopf mould and dust it
with flour. Preheat the oven to 170°C (325°F or Mark
3).

Mix the flour, bicarbonate of soda and sugar in a
bowl. With an electric mixer on the lowest speed, cut
the butter and margarine into the dry ingredients until
the mixture has the consistency of fine meal.

Stir together the vanilla extract, buttermilk and egg
whites. Mix half of this liquid with the dry ingredients
on medium-low speed for 1 minute. Add the remaining liquid and mix it in at medium speed for 1 minute
more, scraping down the sides of the bowl as necessary. Stir in the grated lemon rind.

Pour the batter into the prepared mould. Bake the
cake until it begins to pull away from the sides of the
mould and feels springy to the touch—about 55 minutes. Set the cake aside to cool in the mould.

To make the glaze, combine the sugar, buttermilk
and honey in a small saucepan. Bring the liquid to the
boil over medium heat, then continue boiling it, stirring occasionally, until it is a light caramel colour and
has thickened slightly—about 10 minutes. (Although
the buttermilk in the glaze will separate when the liquid first comes to the boil, the subsequent cooking
will yield a smooth, well-blended sauce.)

Remove the saucepan from the heat; stir in the vanilla extract and 1 teaspoon of water. Let the mixture
cool completely—it should be thick enough to coat
the back of a spoon. Invert the cooled cake on to a
serving platter. Lift away the mould and pour the
glaze over the cake, letting the glaze run down the
sides.

Kugel with Dried Fruit

Serves 12

Working time: about 35 minutes

Total time: about 1 hour and 35 minutes

Calories 325, Protein 13g, Cholesterol 17mg, Total fat 6g,
Saturated fat 3g, Sodium 230mg

250 g/8 oz *dried wide egg noodles*
200 g/7 oz *sugar*
500 g/1 lb *low-fat cottage cheese*
250 g/8 oz *curd cheese*
¹/₄ litre *plain low-fat yoghurt*
1 tsp *pure vanilla extract*
2 tbsp *fresh lemon juice*
150 g/5 oz *sultanas*
75 g/2¹/₂ oz *dried pears, diced*
60 g/2 oz *dried apples, diced*
75 g/2¹/₂ oz *dried stoned prunes, diced*
2 tbsp *cornflour*
¹/₂ litre/16 fl oz *semi-skimmed milk*
2 tbsp *dry breadcrumbs*
Cinnamon topping
30 g/1 oz *unsalted butter, softened*
60 g/2 oz *dry breadcrumbs*
¹/₂ tsp *ground cinnamon*
2 tbsp *sugar*

Add the noodles to 3 litres (5 pints) of boiling water. Start testing for doneness after 7 minutes and continue cooking the noodles until they are *al dente*. Drain the noodles and rinse them under cold running water, then set them aside.

Preheat the oven to 180°C (350°F or Mark 4). In a large bowl, mix together the sugar, cottage cheese, curd cheese, yoghurt, vanilla extract, lemon juice, sultanas, pears, apples and prunes. Dissolve the cornflour in 12.5 cl (4 fl oz) of the milk. Stir the cornflour mixture and the remaining milk into the cheese mixture.

Stir the noodles together with the cheese mixture, coating them well. Lightly oil a non-reactive 23 by 33 cm (9 by 13 inch) baking dish and coat it with the two tablespoons of breadcrumbs. Transfer the noodles to the baking dish.

To make the cinnamon topping, mix together the butter, the breadcrumbs, the cinnamon and the sugar. Sprinkle the topping over the noodles, then cover the dish with foil, and bake it for 30 minutes. Remove the foil and bake the kugel until it is golden-brown about 30 minutes more.

Indian Pudding with Buttermilk Cream

Serves 8

Working time: about 25 minutes

Total time: about 2 hours

Calories 230, Protein 8g, Cholesterol 13mg, Total fat 3g,
Saturated fat 2g, Sodium 125mg

90 g/3 oz *yellow cornmeal*
1 tsp *ground cinnamon*
1 tsp *ground ginger*
1 litre/1³/₄ pints *semi-skimmed milk*
165 g/5¹/₂ oz *molasses*
1 tsp *pure vanilla extract*
Buttermilk cream
2 tbsp *cornflour*
4 tbsp *sugar*
¹/₄ litre/8 fl oz *semi-skimmed milk*
¹/₄ litre/8 fl oz *buttermilk*
1 tsp *pure vanilla extract*

Preheat the oven to 170°C (325°F or Mark 3).

Combine the cornmeal, cinnamon, ginger and ¹/₄ litre (8 fl oz) of the milk in a heatproof bowl. Pour the remaining milk into a saucepan and bring it to the boil. Stirring constantly, pour the hot milk into the cornmeal mixture in a thin, steady stream.

Transfer the cornmeal mixture to the saucepan; stirring continuously, bring it to the boil. Reduce the heat to medium low and cook the mixture, stirring constantly, until it has the consistency of a thick sauce—about 3 minutes more. Stir in the molasses and the vanilla extract, then pour the cornmeal mixture into a baking dish, and bake it until it sets—about 1 hour.

While the pudding is baking, make the buttermilk cream. Mix the cornflour and sugar in a small saucepan, then whisk in the semi-skimmed milk. Bring the mixture to the boil and cook it for 1 minute. Remove the pan from the heat and stir in the buttermilk and vanilla. Transfer the buttermilk cream to a bowl and chill it in the refrigerator.

Remove the pudding from the oven and allow it to cool at room temperature for about 45 minutes; just before serving, top the pudding with the chilled buttermilk cream.

Hot Spiced Fruit Salad

Serves 8

Working (and total) time: about 40 minutes

Calories 160, Protein 1g, Cholesterol 0mg, Total fat 0g,
Saturated fat 0g, Sodium 10mg

1 *orange, rind thinly pared, in one long spiral if possible*
¹/₄ litre/8 fl oz *fresh orange juice*
¹/₂ tsp *ground ginger*
8 *cardamom pods, crushed*
5 cm/2 inch *piece of cinnamon stick*
125 g/4 oz *soft light brown sugar*
1 *mango, peeled, stoned, flesh cut into thin slices*
1 *papaya, cut in half, seeds and skin removed, flesh cut lengthwise into thin slices*
¹/₂ *pineapple, skin removed, flesh cut lengthwise into thin slices, core discarded*
2 *large peaches, blanched for 30 seconds, peeled, stoned and cut into 8 sections*
2 *plums, stoned and quartered*
2 *kiwi fruits, peeled and sliced*

Put the orange rind, orange juice, ginger, cardamom, cinnamon and brown sugar into a large bowl. Stir thoroughly, then microwave the mixture on high for 4 minutes, stirring after 2 minutes.

Add the mango, papaya and pineapple slices to the orange juice mixture and microwave on high for 2 minutes. Add the peaches, plums and kiwi fruits and microwave for a further 3 to 4 minutes, stirring twice, until the fruits are heated through but not overcooked. Serve the fruit salad hot.

Lemon Cornmeal Cake with Blueberry Sauce

Serves 10

Working time: about 35 minutes

Total time: about 1 hour and 30 minutes

Calories 215, Protein 4g, Cholesterol 68mg, Total fat 9g, Saturated fat 4g, Sodium 90mg

2 tbsp	*desiccated coconut*
100 g/3½ oz	*caster sugar*
30 g/1 oz	*blanched almonds*
125 g/4 oz	*cornmeal*
70 g/2½ oz	*plain flour*
1½ tsp	*baking powder*
12.5 cl/4 fl oz	*buttermilk*
1	*lemon, grated rind and juice*
60 g/2 oz	*unsalted butter*
2	*eggs*
300 g/10 oz	*blueberries*
⅛ tsp	*ground cinnamon*

Preheat the oven to 180°C (350°F or Mark 4). Cut pieces of greaseproof paper to fit the bottom and sides of a 23 by 12.5 cm (9 by 5 inch) loaf tin. Line the tin with the greaseproof paper.

Grind the coconut with 1 tablespoon of the sugar in a blender or food processor Transfer the coconut to a small bowl. Grind the almonds with 1 tablespoon of the remaining sugar in the blender or food processor; transfer the almonds to the bowl containing the coconut, and set it aside.

Sift the cornmeal, flour and baking powder into a bowl. Combine the buttermilk, lemon rind and lemon juice in a measuring jug. Cream the butter and the remaining sugar in a bowl; the mixture should be light and fluffy. Add the two eggs, one at a time, to the creamed butter and sugar, beating well after each addition. Fold in the sifted ingredients and the buttermilk alternately, adding a third of each mixture at a time. When the batter is thoroughly mixed, stir in the ground coconut and almonds.

Spoon the batter into the prepared loaf tin. Bake the cake until a wooden toothpick inserted in the centre comes out clean—30 to 40 minutes. Cool the tin on a rack for 10 to 15 minutes, then turn out the cake on the rack. Remove the greaseproof paper; set the cake right side up to cool.

Just before serving time, prepare the blueberry sauce. Combine the blueberries and cinnamon in a small, heavy-bottomed saucepan over medium heat. Cook the blueberries, stirring occasionally, until they pop and exude some of their juice—about 5 minutes. Serve the sauce warm—do not let it cool—with slices of cake.

Lemon-Buttermilk Custards with Candied Lemon Slices

Serves 8

Working time: about 20 minutes

Total time: about 2 hours and 40 minutes
(includes chilling)

Calories 185, Protein 5g, Cholesterol 70mg, Total fat 2g,
Saturated fat 1g, Sodium 115mg

2	*eggs*
200 g/7 oz	*caster sugar*
45 g/1¹/₂ oz	*plain flour*
2 tsp	*pure lemon extract*
³/₄ litre/1¹/₄ pints	*butter milk*
3	*lemons, thinly sliced, for garnish*
60 g/2 oz	*raspberries for garnish*

Preheat the oven to 150°C (300°F or Mark 2).

To prepare the custard, first whisk the eggs in a bowl, then whisk in ↑35 g (4¹/₂ oz) of the sugar and the flour; when the custard is smooth, stir in the lemon extract and buttermilk. Pour the custard into eight 12.5cl (4 fl oz) ramekins and set them on a baking sheet. Bake the custards until they are puffed up and set, and a knife inserted at the edge comes out clean—15 to 20 minutes. Let the custards cool slightly, then refrigerate them until they are well chilled—about 2 hours.

To make the candied lemon slices, lightly oil a baking sheet and set it aside. Combine the remaining sugar with 4 tablespoons of water in a small, heavy-bottomed saucepan. Bring the mixture to the boil, then reduce the heat to low and cook, stirring occasionally, until the sugar has dissolved and the syrup is clear—about 1¹/₂ minutes. Add the lemon slices to the pan; immediately turn the slices over, coating them well, and cook them for about 30 seconds. Transfer the slices to the oiled baking sheet.

To serve, run a small knife round the inside of each ramekin and invert the custards on to serving plates. Garnish each plate with a few candied lemon slices and a sprinkling of fresh raspberries.

Layered Bavarian

Serves 8

Working time: about 1 hour

Total time: about 4 hours and 30 minutes (includes chilling)

Calories 185, Protein 10g, Cholesterol 5mg, Total fat 2g, Saturated fat 1g, Sodium 85mg

500 g/1 lb	ripe apricots or nectarines
1 tbsp	fresh lemon juice
3 tbsp	powdered gelatine
³/₄ litre/1¹/₄ pints	plain low-fat yoghurt
2 tbsp	honey
1 tsp	pure vanilla extract
300 g/10 oz	blackberries, picked over and stemmed
1 tbsp	fresh lime juice
3	egg whites
100 g/3¹/₂ oz	sugar
3	apricots, or 2 nectarines, thinly sliced, for garnish (optional)

Bring 4 litres (7 pints) of water to the boil in a large pan. Add the apricots or nectarines and blanch them until their skins loosen—30 seconds to 1 minute. Remove the apricots or nectarines from the water; when they are cool enough to handle, peel them and cut them in half, discarding the stones and skins. Purée the halves with the lemon juice in a food processor or a blender.

Pour 2 tablespoons of water into a small saucepan. Sprinkle in 1 tablespoon of the gelatine. Heat the mixture over low, heat, stirring continuously until the gelatine has dissolved. Blend the gelatine mixture and 12.5 cl (4 fl oz) of the yoghurt into the fruit purée. Set the mixture aside.

In a bowl, combine ¹/₂ litre (16 fl oz) of the remaining yoghurt with the honey and vanilla. Pour 2 tablespoons of water into a small saucepan and sprinkle in 1 tablespoon of the remaining gelatine. Heat the mixture over low heat to dissolve the gelatine, then whisk it into the yoghurt-honey mixture. Set this mixture aside.

Heat the blackberries and lime juice in a small, non-reactive saucepan over medium heat until the berries render their juice—about 5 minutes. Purée the berries and juice in a food processor or a blender, then strain the purée through a fine sieve.

Pour 2 tablespoons of water into a small saucepan; sprinkle in the remaining tablespoon of gelatine, and

heat the mixture over low heat until the gelatine dissolves. Blend this gelatine mixture and the remaining yoghurt into the blackberry purée. Set the blackberry mixture aside.

Pour the egg whites into a deep bowl. Set up an electric mixer; you will need to start beating the egg whites as soon as the syrup is ready.

To prepare Italian meringue, heat the sugar with 4 tablespoons of water in a small saucepan over medium-high heat. Boil the mixture until the bubbles rise to the surface in a random pattern, indicating that the water has nearly evaporated and the sugar itself is beginning to cook.

With a small spoon, drop a little of the syrup into a bowl of iced water. If the syrup dissolves instantly, continue cooking it. When the syrup dropped into the water can be rolled between your fingers into a supple ball, begin beating the egg whites on high speed. Pour the syrup down the side of the bowl in a thin, steady stream. When all the syrup has been incorporated, decrease the speed to medium; continue beating the egg whites until they are glossy, have formed stiff peaks and have cooled to room temperature—at least 5 minutes. Increase the speed to high and beat the meringue for 1 minute more.

Fold one third of the meringue into each of the prepa red mixtures. Do not refrigerate any of the mixtures.

Rinse a 2 litre (3¹/₂ pint) mould under cold running water. Shake it dry; to facilitate unmoulding the finished dessert, do not wipe it dry. Pour the apricot or nectarine mixture into the mould and refrigerate it for 45 minutes. Next, pour in the vanilla mixture and refrigerate the mould for 45 minutes more. Finally, pour the blackberry mixture into the mould, forming the third layer, and chill in the refrigerator for at least 2 hours.

Unmould the Bavarian as close to serving time as possible: dip the bottom of the mould into hot water for 15 seconds, then run the tip of a knife round the inside edge of the mould to break the air lock. Invert a chilled platter on top, and turn both platter and mould over together. If the Bavarian does not come free, wrap the mould in a towel that has been soaked with hot water and wrung out. After 15 seconds, remove the towel and lift away the mould. If you like, garnish the Bavarian with apricot or nectarine slices.

Layered Marron and Orange Gateau

Serves 10

Working time: about 30 minutes

Total time: about 2 hours and 30 minutes

Calories 230, Protein 5g, Cholesterol 50mg, Total fat 7g, Saturated fat 2g, Sodium 100mg

125 g/4 oz	brown flour
1½ tsp	baking powder
90 g/3 oz	light brown sugar
2 tbsp	safflower oil
2	eggs, yolks and whites separated
1 tsp	grated orange rind
45 g/1½ oz	shelled hazelnuts, toasted and finely chopped
1	orange, skin and pith sliced off, flesh cut into segments

Orange chestnut filling

450 g/15 oz	chestnut purée
1	orange, grated rind only
4 tbsp	plain low-fat yoghurt
1 tbsp	clear honey

Preheat the oven to 180°C (350°F or Mark 4). Grease a deep 20 cm (8 inch) cake tin and line its base with greaseproof paper. Grease and lightly flour the paper.

Sift the flour and baking powder together into a mixing bowl and stir in the sugar. Whisk the oil in a small bowl with the egg yolks, the orange rind and 3 tablespoons of water. Stir the liquid into the flour mixture, then beat with a wooden spoon to make a smooth, glossy batter. In another bowl, whisk the egg whites until stiff but not dry. Add one third of the whites to the batter and fold them in using a spatula or large metal or plastic spoon. Fold in the remaining whites and pour the mixture into the prepared tin. Tap the tin on the work surface to level the mixture.

Bake the cake in the centre of the oven for 25 to 30 minutes, until well risen, lightly browned and springy when touched in the centre. Loosen the edges of the cake with a palette knife and turn it out of the tin on to a wire rack. Remove the lining paper and leave the cake until it has cooled completely.

To make the filling, beat the chestnut purée, orange rind, yoghurt and honey in a bowl with a wooden spoon until smooth. Spoon 2 tablespoons of the filling into a piping bag fitted with a small star nozzle.

Cut the cake into three layers. Put the base layer on a plate and spread its top surface with one quarter of the remaining filling. Stack and spread the other layers in the same way and spread the final quarter of the filling over the sides of the cake. Press the chopped hazelnuts against the sides of the cake to coat them evenly. Arrange the orange segments radiating outwards from the centre of the cake. Pipe stars round the top of the cake and a rosette in the centre.

EDITOR'S NOTE: To obtain 450 g (15 oz) chestnut purée from fresh chestnuts, slit about 1 kg (2 lb) of chestnuts down one side, parboil them for 1 to 2 minutes, shell and peel them. Simmer the chestnuts for about 20 minutes in water, until they are tender. Drain and sieve them. To toast hazelnuts, put them on a baking sheet in a preheated 180°C (350°F or Mark 4) oven for 10 minutes.

Meringue Coffee Torte

Serves 12
Working time: about 50 minutes
Total time: about 2 hours and 30 minutes

Calories 165, Protein 10g, Cholesterol 45mg, Total fat 6g,
Saturated fat 1g, Sodium 220mg

---

30 g/1 oz *light brown sugar*
2 *eggs*
60 g/2 oz *brown flour*
1/2 tsp *baking powder*
300 g/10 oz *skimmed-milk soft cheese*
4 tbsp *double cream*
1 tbsp *clear honey*
3 tsp *strong black coffee*
icing sugar to decorate
18 *walnut halves*
Walnut meringue
2 *egg whites*
90 g/3 oz *demerara sugar*
45 g/1 1/2 oz *shelled walnuts, finely chopped*
2 tsp *cornflour*

Preheat the oven to 180°C (350°F or Mark 4). Grease a 20 cm (8 inch) round cake tin. Line its base with greaseproof paper and grease the paper.

Put the brown sugar and eggs in a bowl set over simmering water. Whisk the mixture by hand or with an electric whisk until thick and pale. Remove the bowl from the heat and whisk until the whisk, when lifted, leaves a trail on the surface. Sift the flour and baking powder together into the mixture. Using a spatula or large metal or plastic spoon, fold in the flour. Pour the mixture into the prepared tin and level the top with a small palette knife.

Bake the sponge in the centre of the oven until risen, lightly coloured and springy when touched in the centre—15 to 20 minutes. Leave the cake in the tin for 5 minutes, then turn it out on to a wire rack. Remove the paper and leave the cake to cool.

To make the walnut meringue, reduce the oven setting to 130°C (250°F or Mark 1/2). Line a baking sheet with non-stick parchment paper. Draw two 18.5 cm (7 1/2 inch) circles on the parchment and invert the parchment. (The meringue circles are smaller than the tin in which the sponge rounds cook because meringue, unlike sponge, does not shrink as it cools.) In a large bowl, whisk the egg whites until they hold stiff peaks. Add one third of the sugar at a time, whisking well after each addition. Mix together the walnuts and cornflour, and fold them into the meringue.

Divide the walnut meringue between the two circles and spread it evenly. Bake the rounds for 1 hour to 1 hour and 20 minutes, until the meringue feels firm and no longer sticky. Transfer the parchment with the meringue rounds to a wire rack. When the meringue is cold, peel off the parchment.

Beat the cheese and cream in a bowl with a wooden spoon. Stir in the honey and coffee. Put 2 tablespoons of the coffee cream in a piping bag fitted with a medium star nozzle.

Place a meringue round on a plate and spread it with one third of the remaining coffee cream. Slice the sponge in half horizontally. Set one layer on the meringue and spread it with another third of the coffee cream. Top the coffee cream with the remaining layer of sponge, the rest of the coffee cream, and finally the second meringue round.

Dust the torte with the icing sugar. Pipe coffee cream scrolls round the top edge of the torte and decorate it with the walnut halves.

Mango Ice Cream

Serves 8

Working time: about 40 minutes

Total time: 1 to 3 hours, depending on freezing method

Calories 155, Protein 3g, Cholesterol 18mg, Total fat 5g,
Saturated fat 3g, Sodium 35mg

1.5 kg/3 lb *ripe mangoes, peeled and stoned*
35 cl/12 fl oz *semi-skimmed milk*
6 tbsp *double cream*
3 tbsp *caster sugar*
1 *lime, juice only*

Cut enough of the mangoes into small cubes to weigh 250 g (8 oz); chill the cubes in the refrigerator.

Purée the remaining mangoes in a blender or a food processor and transfer the purée to a bowl. (There should be about ½ litre/16 fl oz of purée.) Add the milk, cream, sugar and lime juice, and stir until the sugar dissolves. Freeze the ice cream.

Scoop the ice cream into serving dishes, then serve each portion with some of the chilled mango cubes.

Maple Mousse with Glazed Apple Nuggets

Serves 6

Working time: about 1 hour

Total time: about 1 hour and 45 minutes

Calories 215, Protein 2g, Cholesterol 25mg, Total fat 7g,
Saturated fat 4g, Sodium 35mg

---

15 g/¹/₂ oz	*unsalted butter*
2	*tart green apples, peeled, cored and cut into 1 cm (¹/₂ inch) cubes*
1 tsp	*fresh lemon juice*
175 g/6 oz	*maple syrup*
6 tbsp	*double cream*
¹/₂ tsp	*pure vanilla extract*
3	*egg whites, at room temperature*
5 tbsp	*light brown sugar*

Melt the butter in a large, heavy frying pan set over medium-high heat. When the butter is hot, add the apple cubes and lemon juice; sauté the cubes, turning them frequently, until they are light brown—about 10 minutes. Dribble 1 tablespoon of the maple syrup over the apple cubes and sauté them for 1 minute more. Transfer the glazed apple cubes to a plate and refrigerate them.

In a small bowl, whip the cream until it holds stiff peaks, stir in the vanilla extract, then refrigerate the cream. Put the egg whites into a deep bowl and set them aside.

To prepare the maple flavouring for the mousse, combine half of the remaining maple syrup and the sugar in a small, heavy-bottomed saucepan. Bring the mixture to the boil and cook it to the soft-ball stage over medium heat. Begin testing after 4 minutes: with a small spoon, drop a bit of the syrup into a bowl filled with iced water. When the mixture can be rolled into a ball, start beating the egg whites with an electric mixer on medium-high speed. Pour the hot syrup into the whites in a thin, steady stream, beating as you pour. Continue to beat the whites until the meringue has cooled to room temperature—about 7 minutes. Gently fold the whipped cream and the chilled apple pieces into the meringue. (Do not overfold.) Immediately spoon the mousse into six individual dishes and refrigerate them for at least 45 minutes.

To prepare the maple sugar, bring the remaining syrup to the boil in a small, heavy-bottomed saucepan. Reduce the heat to medium and cook the syrup, stirring frequently, until the mixture crystallizes—about 15 minutes. Remove the saucepan from the heat and allow the mixture to cool for 10 minutes, stirring occasionally. Scrape the crystallized sugar out of the pan on to a clean work surface. Using a rolling pin or the bottom of a heavy pan, crush the sugar until it is finely crumbled.

Just before serving, sprinkle some of the maple sugar on to each portion of mousse.

Mile-High Pie with Two Sauces

Serves 12

Working time: about 1 hour

Total time: about 2 hours

Calories 240, Protein 6g, Cholesterol 70mg, Total fat 3g,
Saturated fat 1g, Sodium 85mg

1 tbsp *safflower oil*
315 g/10¹/₂ oz *caster sugar*
12 *egg whites*
1 tbsp *pure vanilla extract*
¹/₄ tsp *cream of tartar*

Vanilla-yoghurt sauce

30 cl/¹/₂ pint *semi-skimmed milk*
1 *vanilla pod*
3 *egg yolks*
2 tbsp *caster sugar*
¹/₄ litre/8 fl oz *plain low-fat yoghurt*

Cranberry sauce

200 g/7 oz *fresh or frozen cranberries, picked over*
100 g/3¹/₂ oz *caster sugar*
12.5 cl/4 fl oz *ruby port*
6 tbsp *plain low-fat yoghurt*

Brush the inside of a 23 cm (9 inch) spring form tin with the oil. Sprinkle in 15 g (¹/₂ oz) of the sugar; shake and tilt the pan to coat it evenly with the sugar. Preheat the oven to 150°C (300°F or Mark 2).

To prepare the meringue, put the egg whites, vanilla extract and cream of tartar into a bowl. Begin beating the whites at low speed, gradually increasing the speed to medium as the whites turn opaque. Add the remaining 300 g (10 oz) of sugar a tablespoon at a time, increasing the beater speed all the while. When all the sugar has been incorporated, continue beating the whites on high speed until they are glossy and form stiff peaks when the beater is lifted from the bowl.

Transfer the meringue to the spring form tin. Smooth the top of the meringue with a long spatula or the dull side of a knife. Bake the pie until it has risen and is lightly browned—about 40 minutes. It will be moist throughout. Remove the pie from the oven and let it cool to room temperature in the tin.

While the pie is baking and cooling, make the sauces. To make the vanilla-yoghurt sauce, heat the milk, vanilla pod, egg yolks and sugar in a small, heavy-bottomed, non-reactive saucepan set over low heat. Cook the mixture, stirring constantly with a wooden spoon, until it is thick enough to coat the back of the spoon. Strain the sauce into a bowl and set it aside; when it has cooled to room temperature, whisk in the yoghurt.

To make the cranberry sauce, cook the cranberries, sugar and 12.5 cl (4 fl oz) of water in a small saucepan over medium-high heat. Cook the cranberries until they burst—6 to 8 minutes. Continue cooking the berries until they are quite soft—about 5 minutes. Press the cooked berries through a sieve into a bowl and set them aside. When they have cooled to room temperature, whisk in the port and the yoghurt.

Just before serving the pie, remove the sides of the tin. With a wet knife, cut the pie into wedges; present them with the vanilla-yoghurt sauce and the cranberry sauce poured round them. If you like, swirl the two sauces together as shown below.

Mocha Pudding

Serves 6

Working time: about 20 minutes

Total time: about 1 hour and 20 minutes (includes chilling)

Calories 220, Protein 5g, Cholesterol 11mg, Total fat 7g,
Saturated fat 4g, Sodium 110mg

45 g/^{1}/$_2$ oz *plain chocolate*
60 cl/1 pint *semi-skimmed milk*
12.5 cl/4 fl oz *double-strength coffee*
4 tbsp *cornflour*
150 g/5 oz *caster sugar*
^{1}/$_8$ tsp *salt*
3 tbsp *half cream, half milk*

Place the chocolate in a 2 litre (3^1/$_2$ pint) glass bowl and cook it on medium (50 per cent power) for 2 to 3 minutes. (Though the chocolate will appear not to have melted, it will be soft.) Whisk the milk and coffee into the chocolate. Combine the cornflour, sugar and salt, and whisk them into the milk mixture. Microwave the contents of the bowl on high for 4 minutes. Whisk the mixture and continue cooking it on high, whisking every 60 seconds, until it thickens—4 to 6 minutes more. Pour the pudding into six dessert cups and refrigerate them for at least 1 hour.

Just before serving the pudding, dribble ^{1}/$_2$ tablespoon of the cream-milk mixture over each portion.

Orange Chiffon Cheesecake

Serves 12

Working time: about 1 hour

Total time: about 1 day (includes chilling)

Calories 145, Protein 7g, Cholesterol 12mg, Total fat 4g,
Saturated fat 2g, Sodium 130mg

200 g/7 oz	*sugar*
2	*oranges, halved lengthwise and cut crosswise into 3mm (⅛ inch) slices*
12.5 cl/4 fl oz	*fresh orange juice*
2½ tbsp	*fresh lemon juice*
2½ tsp	*powdered gelatine*
250 g/8 oz	*low-fat ricotta cheese*
225 g/7½ oz	*low-fat cottage cheese*
60 g/2 oz	*low-fat creamy soft cheese*
1	*orange, grated rind only*
1	*lemon, grated rind only*
3	*egg whites*

Put the sugar and 12.5 cl (4 fl oz) of water into a saucepan. Bring the mixture to the boil, then add the orange slices, reduce the heat, and simmer the oranges for 20 minutes. Refrigerate the oranges in the syrup for 1 hour.

Pour the orange juice and lemon juice into a small saucepan. Sprinkle in the gelatine, then set the pan aside until the gelatine has softened.

Meanwhile, purée the ricotta, cottage cheese, soft cheese, orange rind and lemon rind in a food processor or a blender until the mixture is very smooth. Transfer the cheese mixture to a bowl.

Set the saucepan containing the gelatine mixture over low heat; cook it, stirring continuously, until the gelatine has dissolved. Stir the gelatine mixture into the puréed cheeses.

Remove the orange slices from their syrup and drain them on paper towels. Reserve the syrup.

Pour the egg whites into a deep bowl. Set up an electric mixer; you will need to start beating the egg whites as soon as the syrup is ready.

To prepare Italian meringue, heat the reserved syrup in a small saucepan over medium-high heat until it boils. Continue to boil the mixture until the bubbles rise to the surface in a random pattern, indicating that the liquid has nearly evaporated and the sugar itself is beginning to cook.

With a small spoon, drop a little of the syrup into a bowl filled with iced water. If the syrup dissolves immediately, continue cooking the syrup mixture. When the syrup dropped into the water can be rolled between your fingers into a supple ball, begin beating the egg whites on high speed. Pour the syrup down the side of the bowl in a very thin, steady stream. When all the syrup has been incorporated, decrease the speed to medium; continue beating the egg whites until they are glossy, have formed stiff peaks and have cooled to room temperature. Increase the speed to high and beat the meringue for 1 minute more.

Mix about one quarter of the meringue into the cheese mixture to lighten it, then gently fold in the rest. Rinse a 1.5 litre (2½ pint) ring mould with cold water and shake out the excess. (Do not wipe the mould dry; the clinging moisture will help the dessert unmould cleanly.) Line the mould with the drained orange slices, then pour in the cheesecake mixture, and chill it in the refrigerator for 4 hours.

To turn out the cheesecake, invert a chilled platter on top of the mould and turn both over together. Wrap the bottom of the mould in a towel that has been soaked with hot water and wrung out. After 5 seconds, remove the towel and lift away the mould.

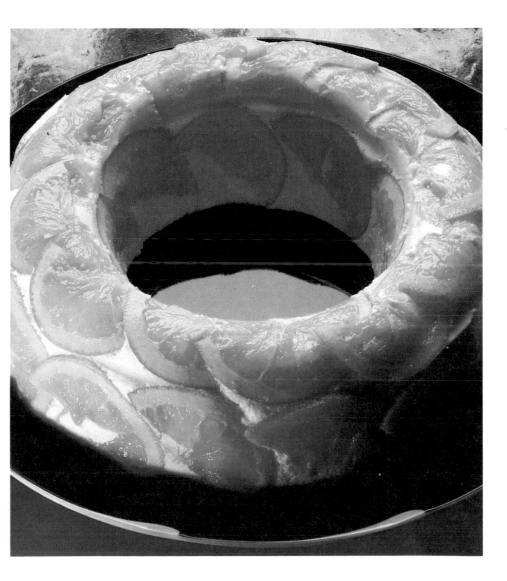

Orange-Beetroot Cake

Serves 16

Working time: about 1 hour

Total time: about 1 hour and 45 minutes

Calories 190, Protein 3g, Cholesterol 50mg, Total fat 6g, Saturated fat 1g, Sodium 115mg

45 g/1¹/₂ oz	*sultanas*
45 g/1¹/₂ oz	*raisins*
¹/₄ litre/8 fl oz	*fresh orange juice*
100 g/3¹/₂ oz	*plain flour*
90 g/3 oz	*wholemeal flour*
1 tsp	*bicarbonate of soda*
¹/₄ tsp	*salt*
1 tsp	*ground cinnamon*
1 tsp	*grated nutmeg*
3	*eggs, separated, the whites at room temperature*
6 tbsp	*safflower oil*
1 tbsp	*grated orange rind*
1 tsp	*pure vanilla extract*
75 g/2¹/₂ oz	*dark brown sugar*
6 tbsp	*plain low-fat yoghurt*
3	*raw beetroots, peeled and grated*
135 g/4¹/₂ oz	*caster sugar*

Put the sultanas, raisins and orange juice into a non-reactive saucepan. Bring the juice to the boil, then reduce the heat and simmer the mixture for 5 minutes. Drain the sultanas and raisins in a sieve set over another non-reactive saucepan; reserve the juice and set the sultanas and raisins aside. Return the juice to

the heat and simmer it until only about 3 tablespoons remain—7 minutes or so.

Preheat the oven to 180°C (350°F or Mark 4).

Lightly oil a 23 cm (9 inch) springform tin. Line the base of the tin with a disc of greaseproof paper, then lightly oil the paper, and dust the tin with flour.

Sift the plain flour, wholemeal flour, bicarbonate of soda, salt, cinnamon and nutmeg into a bowl. In a separate bowl, whisk the egg yolks. Stir 1 tablespoon of the oil into the yolks. Whisking vigorously, blend in the remaining oil a tablespoon at a time. Continue whisking the yolks until the mixture is emulsified. Stir the orange rind, vanilla extract, brown sugar, yoghurt, beetroot, sultanas and raisins into the yolk mixture. Fold the flour mixture into the yolk mixture.

Beat the egg whites until soft peaks form. Sprinkle in the caster sugar and beat for 1 minute more. Stir one quarter of the beaten egg whites into the batter to lighten it, then gently fold the lightened batter into the remaining beaten egg whites. Pour the batter mixture into the prepared springform tin.

Bake the cake just until a knife inserted in the centre comes out clean—45 to 55 minutes. Remove the cake from the oven and let it cool for 10 minutes. Gently reheat the reserved orange juice and brush it over the top of the warm cake.

EDITOR'S NOTE: This cake tastes even better two or three days after it has been baked. Store it in an airtight container.

Papaya Porcupines with Coconut Quills

Makes about 20 porcupines
Working time: about 30 minutes
Total time: about 45 minutes
Per porcupine: Calories 50, Protein 1g, Cholesterol 0mg,
Total fat 1g, Saturated fat 1g, Sodium 14mg

2	*egg whites*
2 tbsp	*fresh lemon juice*
75 g/2¹/₂ oz	*plain flour*
6 tbsp	*caster sugar*
60 g/2 oz	*shredded coconut*
1	*papaya (about 500 g/1lb), peeled and cut into about 20 chunks*

Preheat the oven to 200°C (400°F or Mark 6).

Prepare the coating for the papaya: in a small bowl, thoroughly whisk the egg whites, lemon juice, flour and 2 tablespoons of the sugar. Set aside. Spread out the coconut on a sheet of greaseproof paper.

Toss the papaya pieces with the remaining sugar. Dip a piece of papaya into the coating, then hold the piece over the bowl and allow the excess coating to drip off. Roll the papaya piece in the coconut, then transfer it to a baking sheet. Repeat the process to coat the remaining pieces.

Bake the papaya porcupines until the coating has set and is lightly browned—about 15 minutes. Serve the papaya porcupines warm.

Pears with a Spiced Walnut Crust

Serves 10

Working time: about 40 minutes

Total time: about 1 hour and 20 minutes

Calories 285, Protein 3g, Cholesterol 6mg, Total fat 9g,
Saturated fat 2g, Sodium 35mg

60 g/2 oz	*shelled walnuts*
150 g/5 oz	*plain flour*
6 tbsp	*light brown sugar*
30 g/1 oz	*unsalted butter*
30 g/1 oz	*polyunsaturated margarine*
1/4 tsp	*ground mace*
1/4 tsp	*ground ginger*
1	*lemon, grated rind only*
1/2 tsp	*pure vanilla extract*
6	*pears*
300 g/10 oz	*red currant jelly or apricot jam*

Preheat the oven to 190°C (375°F or Mark 5).

Spread the walnuts on a baking sheet and toast them in the oven until their skins begin to pull away—about 10 minutes. Then allow the walnuts to cool to room temperature.

Put the toasted walnuts, flour, brown sugar, butter, margarine, mace, ginger and lemon rind into a food processor. Process the mixture until it resembles coarse meal. Sprinkle the vanilla and 1 tablespoon of water over the mixture, and process it in short bursts just until it begins to hold together in dough pieces about 2.5 cm (1 inch) in diameter. (Do not overprocess the dough lest it form a ball.)

Transfer the pieces of dough to a clean work surface. Rub the pieces between your fingers to finish blending the dough, then put the pieces into a 23 cm (9 inch) tart tin with a removable bottom. Spread out the dough with your fingers, coating the bottom and sides of the tin with a very thin layer; crimp the top edge of the dough with your fingers. Put the tin into the refrigerator.

Peel, halve, and core the pears. Thinly slice each pear half crosswise, then arrange 10 of the pear halves around the edge of the tart shell, pointing their narrow ends towards the centre. Flatten each half, slightly spreading out the slices. Arrange the two remaining halves in the centre of the tart.

Bake the tart until the edges are browned and any juices rendered by the pears have evaporated—about 40 minutes. Set the tart aside to cool.

Cook the jelly or jam in a small saucepan over medium-low heat until it melts—about 4 minutes. If using jam, sieve it. Using a pastry brush, glaze the cooled pears with a thin coating of the melted jelly.

EDITOR'S NOTE: If you do not have a food processor, grind the walnuts in a blender together with 1 tablespoon of sugar, then prepare the dough in a bowl with a pastry blender and a wooden spoon.

Raspberry Roll

THE CREAM CHEESE FILLING FOR THIS CAKE WOULD MELT IF THE CAKE WERE FILLED AND ROLLED IMMEDIATELY IT CAME OUT OF THE OVEN. SO THAT THE SPONGE SETS IN THE FORM OF A ROLL, IT IS ROLLED ROUND A SHEET OF PAPER WHEN HOT. WHEN THE SPONGE IS COOL BUT STILL FLEXIBLE, IT IS SPREAD WITH THE FILLING AND ROLLED UP AGAIN.

Serves 12

Working time: about 40 minutes

Total time: about 1 hour and 15 minutes

Calories 110, Protein 5g, Cholesterol 55mg, Total fat 4g, Saturated fat 2g, Sodium 50mg

2 eggs
60 g/2 oz *light brown sugar*
90 g/3 oz *brown flour*
¹/₂ tsp *baking powder*
30 g/1 oz *fine oatmeal*
2 *egg whites*
¹/₂ tbsp *caster sugar*
175 g/6 oz *cream cheese*
2 tbsp *plain low-fat yoghurt*
2 tsp *clear honey*
125 g/4 oz *fresh raspberries, or frozen raspberries, thawed*
60 g/2 oz *icing sugar*

Preheat the oven to 180°C (350°F or Mark 4). Grease a 32 by 22 cm (13 by 9 inch) Swiss roll tin. Line it with greaseproof paper and grease the paper.

Put the eggs and brown sugar in a bowl set over a pan of hot, but not boiling, water. Whisk by hand or with an electric mixer until the mixture is thick and creamy. Remove the bowl from the saucepan and continue to whisk until the whisk, when lifted, leaves a trail on the surface of the mixture. Sift the flour with the baking powder into another bowl, and mix in the oatmeal. In a third bowl, whisk the egg whites until they are stiff but not dry. Fold the flour and oatmeal mixture, together with one third of the egg whites, into the whisked eggs and sugar. Then fold in the remaining egg whites.

Pour the mixture into the prepared tin and tap the tin against the work surface to level the batter. Bake the sponge in the centre of the oven for 10 to 15 minutes until well risen, lightly browned and springy when touched in the centre.

Place a piece of greaseproof paper on the work surface and sprinkle it with the caster sugar. Invert the sponge on to the sugar. Working quickly, detach the lining paper from the sponge. Trim away the crisp edges on all four sides of the sponge. Cover the sponge with a clean sheet of greaseproof paper and roll up the cake with the paper inside. Transfer the roll to a wire rack to cool.

In a bowl, mix the cream cheese with the yoghurt and honey. Reserve 4 raspberries and gently fold the rest of the raspberries into the cream cheese mixture. As soon as the sponge is cool, unroll it and remove the paper. Spread the raspberry filling evenly over the cake to within 5 mm (¹/₂ inch) of the short sides and right to the edge of the long sides. Roll up the cake tightly and place it on a serving plate.

Sift the icing sugar into a bowl and mix in 1 tablespoon of boiling water. Press one of the reserved raspberries through a nylon sieve set over the bowl, and stir the juice into the icing to colour it pale pink. Beat the icing until it is smooth and glossy. Dribble the icing over the roll. Halve the remaining raspberries and distribute them over the cake. Serve the raspberry roll when the icing has set.

Raspberry Soufflés

Serves 6

Working time: about 30 minutes

Total time: about 1 hour and 10 minutes

Calories 45, Protein 0g, Cholesterol 0mg, Total fat 0g,
Saturated fat 0g, Sodium 6mg

---

125 g/4 oz *caster sugar*
250 g/8 oz *fresh or frozen whole raspberries, thawed*
2 *egg whites*
6 tbsp *icing sugar*

Lightly butter six 12.5 cl (4 fl oz) ramekins. Divide 2 tablespoons of the sugar evenly among the ramekins, then tilt and rotate the ramekins to coat them thoroughly with the sugar. Set the ramekins on a baking sheet and refrigerate them.

Purée the raspberries in a food processor or a blender. Strain the purée through a fine sieve and set it aside. Preheat the oven to 200°C (400°F or Mark 6).

Pour the egg whites into a deep bowl. Set up an electric mixer; you will need to start beating the egg whites as soon as the syrup is ready.

To prepare Italian meringue, heat the remaining sugar with 4 tablespoons of water in a small saucepan over medium-high heat. Boil the mixture until the bubbles rise to the surface in a random pattern, indicating that the water has nearly evaporated and the sugar itself is beginning to cook.

With a small spoon, drop a little of the syrup into a bowl of iced water. If the syrup dissolves immediately, continue cooking. When the syrup dropped into the water can be rolled between your fingers into a supple ball, begin beating the egg whites on high speed. Pour the syrup down the side of the bowl in a very thin, steady stream. When all the syrup has been incorporated, decrease the speed to medium; continue beating the egg whites until they are glossy, have formed stiff peaks and have cooled to room temperature—5 to 10 minutes. Increase the speed to high and beat the meringue for 1 minute more.

Stir about one third of the meringue into the raspberry purée to lighten it, then fold in the remaining meringue. Divide the soufflé mixture among the prepared ramekins, slightly overfilling each one. Level their tops with a spatula, then run the tip of your thumb round the inside edge of each ramekin; the resulting circular depression will keep the edges of the soufflés from burning as the depressions puff up in the oven. Sift 1 tablespoon of the icing sugar over the top of each soufflé; bake the soufflés until they have risen and are set—about 10 minutes. Serve the soufflés immediately.

EDITOR'S NOTE: If it is inconvenient to serve the finished soufflés at once, keep them from collapsing by leaving them in the oven with the heat turned off and the door open.

Rhubarb Tartlets Topped with Meringue

Serves 4

Working (and total) time: about 1 hour and 30 minutes

Calories 200, Protein 3g, Cholesterol 7mg, Total fat 5g, Saturated fat 2g, Sodium 180mg

1	*tart green apple, peeled, cored and cut into 1 cm (1/2 inch) cubes*
2 tbsp	*dry white wine*
500 g/1 lb	*fresh rhubarb, trimmed and cut into 1 cm (1/2 inch) pieces, or frozen rhubarb, thawed*
4 tbsp	*light brown sugar*
1/4 tsp	*pure vanilla extract*
1/2 tsp	*fresh lemon juice*
1/4 tsp	*ground cinnamon*
1/4 tsp	*grated nutmeg*
1/8 tsp	*salt*
4	*sheets frozen phyllo (minimum width 25 cm/10 inches) in a stack, thawed*
15 g/1/2 oz	*unsalted butter, melted.*
1	*egg white*
1 1/2 tbsp	*caster sugar*

Put the apple cubes and wine into a saucepan and simmer them, covered, for 5 minutes. Add the rhubarb, reduce the heat to low, and cook the mixture, uncovered, for 5 minutes more. Stir in the brown sugar, vanilla, lemon juice, cinnamon, a pinch of nutmeg and the salt. Continue cooking the mixture, stirring occasionally, until most of the liquid has evaporated—5 to 10 minutes. Set the mixture aside.

Preheat the oven to 180°C (350°F or Mark 4).

To prepare the pastry, fold the stack of phyllo sheets in half, then fold it in half again and trim off the edges so as to produce a stack of sixteen 12.5 cm (5 inch) squares. Lay one of the phyllo squares on a work surface, using a pastry brush, lightly dab the square with a little of the melted butter. Set a second square on top of the first and brush it with butter. Set a third square on top of the second at a 45-degree angle, forming an eight-pointed star. Dab the top of the third square with butter and cover it with a fourth square.

Lightly oil four cups of a muffin tin. Transfer the stacked phyllo to one of the cups and gently press it in place, taking care that the edges of the phyllo come as far as possible up the sides of the cup. Prepare the remaining phyllo squares in the same manner, making four tartlets in all.

Bake the tartlets until they are light brown and crisp—about 8 minutes. Remove the muffin tin from the oven and unmould the tartlets, then set them aside. Let the tartlets cool to room temperature.

Increase the oven temperature to 240°C (475°F or Mark 9).

To make the meringue, beat the egg white in a small bowl until the white forms soft peaks. Continue beating, gradually adding the sugar, until stiff peaks form when the beater is lifted from the bowl.

Set the tartlets on a baking sheet and divide the rhubarb mixture among them. Using a piping bag or a spoon, top each with some of the meringue; bake the tartlets until the meringue browns—about 3 minutes. Serve the tartlets within 2 hours.

Rhubarb-Gingerbread
Upside-Down Cake

Serves 8

Working time: about 20 minutes

Total time: about 50 minutes

Calories 200, Protein 4g, Cholesterol 40mg, Total fat 4g,
Saturated fat 2g, Sodium 200mg

30 g/1 oz *unsalted butter*
6 tbsp *lightbrown sugar*
250 g/8 oz *fresh rhubarb, coarsely chopped, or frozen
rhubarb, thawed, coarsely chopped*
140 g/5 oz *plain flour*
60 g/2 oz *wholemeal flour*
1 tsp *bicarbonate of soda*
1 tsp *ground ginger*
1 tsp *ground cinnamon*
¹/₂ tsp *grated nutmeg*
¹/₄ tsp *dry mustard*
¹/₄ tsp *ground cloves*
¹/₄ tsp *salt*
1 *egg*
165 g/5¹/₂ oz *dark molasses*
1 tsp *pure vanilla extract*

Put the butter into a 23 cm (9 inch) glass pie plate and microwave it on high for 45 seconds. Smear it over the bottom of the plate, coating it evenly, then sprinkle in the brown sugar Scatter the rhubarb over the sugar.

In a large bowl, combine the plain flour, wholemeal flour, bicarbonate of soda, ginger, cinnamon, nutmeg, mustard, cloves and salt. In a second bowl, mix the egg, molasses, vanilla and 12.5 cl (4 fl oz) of hot water

Stir the liquid into the dry ingredients, forming a smooth batter. Pour the batter to the pie plate and microwave it on high for 10 minutes, turning the dish every 3 minutes.

Remove the cake from the oven and let it stand for 5 minutes. Run the tip of a knife round the sides of the cake Invert a serving plate on top of the pie plate and turn both over together, do not remove the pie plate. Let the cake stand for 5 minutes more, then lift away the pie plate The cake is best served warm.

EDITOR'S NOTE: This cake is also an ideal showcase for other fruits. Coarsely chopped plums, sour cherries' or peeled pears might be substituted for the rhubarb.

Rolled Cherry-Walnut Cake

Serves 8

Working time: about 1 hour

Total time: about 1 hour and 30 minutes

Calories 140, Protein 5g, Cholesterol 70mg, Total fat 4g,
Saturated fat 1g, Sodium 70mg

30 g/1 oz	shelled walnuts, finely chopped
1¹/₂ tbsp	plain flour
¹/₂ tsp	baking powder
2	eggs, separated, plus 1 egg white, the whites at room temperature
2 tbsp	dark brown sugar
¹/₂ tsp	pure vanilla extract
4 tbsp	caster sugar
2 tsp	icing sugar

Cherry filling

¹/₂ tsp	pure vanilla extract
¹/₄ litre/8 fl oz	plain low-fat yoghurt
2 tbsp	caster sugar
250 g/8 oz	fresh cherries, stoned and quartered

Dot the corners and centre of a baking sheet with butter. Line the sheet with greaseproof paper—the butter will hold the paper in place. Lightly butter top of the paper, then dust it with flour and set the pan aside. Heat the oven to 180°C (350°F or Mark 4).

Mix together the walnuts, flour and baking powder in a small bowl; set the mixture aside.

Beat the two egg yolks with the brown sugar and 1¹/₂ tablespoons of very hot water until the mixture is thick enough to fall in a ribbon when the beater is lifted from the bowl—about 4 minutes. Stir in the vanilla and set the bowl aside.

Beat the three egg whites on medium speed in a bowl until they form soft peaks. Increase the speed to medium high and continue beating, gradually adding the caster sugar, until stiff peaks form.

Stir about one quarter of the egg whites into the yolk mixture to lighten it. Gently fold one third of the remaining egg whites into the yolk mixture, then fold in half of the nut-and-flour mixture, followed by half of the remaining egg whites. Finally, fold in the remaining nut-and-flour mixture and the last of the egg whites.

Transfer the batter to the baking sheet and spread it out, forming a rectangle about 28 by 18 cm (11 by 7 inches). Bake the cake until it is lightly browned and springy to the touch—about 20 minutes. Let the cake cool completely—at least 30 minutes.

Sprinkle a sheet of greaseproof paper with icing sugar and invert the cake on to the paper. Gently remove the paper on which the cake baked from the bottom of the cake. Trim the edges of the cake with a serrated knife or scissors. For the filling, stir the vanilla extract into the yoghurt, then spread this mixture on to the cake, leaving a 1 cm (¹/₂ inch) border uncovered all round. Sprinkle the caster sugar over the yoghurt mixture, then scatter the cherries evenly on top. Starting at a long side, roll the cake into a cylinder. Set the cake on a platter; sprinkle the icing sugar over the top just before serving.

Strawberry Cognac Layer Cake

Serves 10
Working time: about 1 hour
Total time: about 10 hours

Calories 175, Protein 8g, Cholesterol 60mg, Total fat 7g,
Saturated fat 3g, Sodium 145mg

2	eggs
1	egg white
90 g/3 oz	vanilla-flavoured caster sugar
90 g/3 oz	plain flour
3 tbsp	cognac
5 tbsp	skimmed milk
6 tbsp	whipping cream

Strawberry filling

250 g/8 oz	cottage cheese, sieved
3 tbsp	skimmed milk
2 tbsp	clear honey
1	lemon, grated rind only
1 tbsp	fresh lemon juice
1¹/₂ tsp	powdered gelatine
250 g/8 oz	strawberries

Preheat the oven to 190°C (375°F or Mark 5). Line a loaf tin approximately 22 by 11 cm (9 by 4¹/₂ inches) and a shallow rectangular tin approximately 32 by 22 cm (13 by 9 inches) with non-stick parchment paper.

Put the eggs, egg white and sugar in a bowl set over a pan of gently simmering water. Whisk with a hand whisk or electric beater until the mixture is very thick and the whisk leaves a heavy trail when lifted. Remove the mixture from the heat and whisk it until it is cool . Sift the flour twice and fold it quickly and evenly into the egg mixture with a metal spoon. Turn the batter into the shallow rectangular tin and level the top. Cook the sponge for 12 to 15 minutes, until well risen and firm to the touch. Turn it out on to a wire rack; leave until cold, then peel off the paper.

Meanwhile, make the filling. Put the cottage cheese, milk, honey and lemon rind in a bowl and beat them with a wooden spoon. Put the lemon juice in a small bowl and stand it in a pan of gently simmering water, then add the gelatine and leave it to dissolve. Stir the gelatine into the cheese mixture. Slice half the strawberries and add them to the mixture.

Cut lengthwise and across the rectangle of sponge to obtain a piece that fits the base of the loaf tin. Set it in position. Combine the cognac and the 5 tablespoons of milk and pour 3 tablespoons over the cake in the tin. When the strawberry-cheese mixture begins to thicken, spoon half into the loaf tin. Cut a second piece of sponge, slightly larger than the first, and use it to cover the strawberry-cheese mixture. Soak the sponge with half of the remaining cognac and milk, and spoon in the rest of the strawberry-cheese mixture. From the piece of sponge that remains, cut enough to cover the second strawberry-cheese layer. Moisten it with the rest of the cognac and milk. Cover the cake with non-stick parchment paper and a rectangle of cardboard to distribute weight. Set a 500 g to 1 kg (1 to 2 lb) weight on the cake and refrigerate overnight; long chilling makes it firm and easy to slice.

Just before serving the cake, turn it out and peel off the paper. Whip the cream until stiff and spread 1 tablespoon over the cake. Spoon the remainder into a piping bag fitted with a large star nozzle. Pipe diagonal lines across the cake top, stars round the base. Slice or halve the remaining strawberries; arrange them round the base and between the lines of cream.

Strawberry Trifle Gateau

Serves 8

Working time: about 35 minutes

Total time: about 6 hours (includes chilling)

Calories 240, Protein 10g, Cholesterol 90mg, Total fat 3g,
Saturated fat 1g, Sodium 50mg

---

3 *eggs*
1 *egg white*
200 g/7 oz *caster sugar*
125 g/4 oz *plain flour*
750 g/1½ lb *fresh strawberries 500g (1 lb) hulled and thinly sliced, the rest reserved for decoration*
250 g/8 oz *quark*
1 tsp *pure vanilla extract*
1 tsp *icing sugar*
15 g/½ oz *shelled pistachio nuts, skinned and thinly sliced*

Heat the oven to 180°C (350°F or Mark 4). Lightly oil a 22 cm (10 inch) springform tin or cake tin. Line the base with greaseproof paper.

Put the whole eggs and egg white into a large bowl with 125 g (4 oz) of the caster sugar and prepare the sponge mixture as demonstrated on the left. Pour the mixture into the prepared tin and spread it evenly. Bake for 25 to 30 minutes, until very lightly browned

and springy to the touch. Leave the sponge to cool slightly in the tin for a few minutes, then carefully turn it out on to a wire rack to cool completely.

Meanwhile, put the sliced strawberries into a bowl with 50 g (2 oz) of the caster sugar. Mix well, cover and leave to stand for about 1½ hours, to allow the strawberries to soften and the sugar to draw out the juice. Blend the quark with the remaining sugar and vanilla.

Cut the cooled sponge in half horizontally. Place the bottom layer on a flat plate. Fit an expanding ring snugly round it (or, alternatively, a deep band of double thickness foil) in order to retain the shape. Spoon half the sliced strawberries and their juice over the sponge layer, then spread on the quark. Spoon the remaining sliced strawberries on top of the quark. Place the second sponge layer on top of the strawberries. Cover the sponge with plastic film and put a flat plate on top. Place some large weights or cans on top of the plate to weight down the gateau. Refrigerate for at least 4 hours, or overnight.

To serve, remove the weights, plate and plastic film. Carefully remove the ring. Slice the reserved strawberries, and use them to decorate the gateau. Sift on the icing sugar and sprinkle the top with the sliced pistachios. Keep refrigerated until ready to serve.

Tangerine Chiffon Cake with Lemon Glaze

Serves 16

Working time about 30 minutes

Total time about 3 hours (includes cooling)

Calories 200, Protein 3g, Cholesterol 70mg, Total fat 6g, Saturated fat 1g, Sodium 110mg

250 g/8 oz	*plain flour*
1 tbsp	*baking powder*
4	*eggs, separated, plus 3 egg whites*
6 tbsp	*safflower oil*
265 g/8¹/₄ oz	*caster sugar*
2¹/₂ tbsp	*finely chopped tangerine rind or grated orange rind*
¹/₄ litre/8 fl oz	*strained tangerine juice or orange juice, preferably fresh*
¹/₂ tsp	*cream of tartar*

Lemon glaze

90 g/3 oz	*icing sugar*
1 tbsp	*fresh lemon juice*
1 tbsp	*grated lemon rind*
1 tbsp	*soured cream*

Preheat the oven to 170°C (325°F or Mark 3)

To make the cake batter, sift the flour and baking powder into a large bowl Whisk in the egg yolks, oil, 135 g (4¹/₂ oz) of the sugar, and the tangerine or orange rind and juice, and mix them thoroughly.

To prepare the meringue, beat the whites and cream of tartar together in another bowl until the whites hold soft peaks. Add the remaining sugar 2 tablespoons at time, beating continuously until the whites are shiny and hold stiff peaks.

Stir one third of the meringue into the cake batter to lighten it, then fold in the remaining meringue. Rinse a 25 cm (10 inch) kugelhopf mould or tube cake tin with water and shake it out so that only a few droplets remain. Spoon the batter into the mould and bake the cake for 50 minutes. Increase the oven temperature to 180°C (350°F or Mark 4) and continue baking the cake until a skewer inserted in the thickest part comes out clean—5 to 15 minutes more.

When the cake is done, remove it from the oven and let it rest for 10 minutes. Loosen it from the sides of the mould with a spatula and invert it on to a rack. Allow the cake to cool completely about 1¹/₂ hours.

To prepare the lemon glaze, first sift the icing sugar into a small bowl, then stir in the lemon juice and rind. Continue stirring until a smooth paste results Stir in the soured cream and pour the glaze over the cake, letting the excess cascade down the sides.

Vanilla Custard with Yoghurt and Apricots

Serves 10

Working time: about 30 minutes

Total time: about 1 hour and 30 minutes (includes chilling)

Calories 205, Protein 6g, Cholesterol 65mg, Total fat 3g,
Saturated fat 2g, Sodium 110mg

125 g/4 oz *dried apricots, coarsely chopped*
200 g/7 oz *plus 1 tbsp sugar*
6 tbsp *cornflour*
1/8 tsp *salt*
1 litre/1³/₄ pints *semi-skimmed milk*
5 cm/2 inch *length of vanilla pod, split lengthwise,*
  or 1 tsp pure vanilla extract
2 *eggs, beaten*
17.5 cl/6 fl oz *plain low-fat yoghurt*

Combine the apricots with 12.5 cl (4 fl oz) of water and 1 tablespoon of the sugar in a glass bowl. Cover the bowl and microwave the mixture on high, stopping midway to stir it, until the apricots are tender—4 to 6 minutes. Purée the mixture in a food processor or a blender, then return the purée to the bowl. Cover the bowl and refrigerate it.

Combine the cornflour, salt and the remaining sugar in a small bowl. Pour the milk into a 2 litre (3¹/₂ pint) glass bowl and add the cornflour mixture. Whisk the mixture until the cornflour is completely dissolved. Add the vanilla pod, if you are using it. Microwave the mixture on high, stopping once or twice to stir it, until the milk is hot—about 8 minutes.

If you are using the vanilla pod, remove it from the milk and scrape the seeds inside it into the milk. Discard the pod.

Whisk about 12.5 cl (4 fl oz) of the hot milk into the eggs. Immediately whisk the egg-milk mixture—and the vanilla extract, if you are using it—into the remaining hot milk. Microwave the mixture on high for 3 minutes. Whisk the mixture and continue cooking it on high, whisking every 60 seconds, until it thickens— 2 to 3 minutes more. Divide the custard among 10 dessert cups and put them into the refrigerator for at least 1 hour.

Just before serving, spread a dollop of yoghurt over each custard and top it with the apricot purée.

EDITOR'S NOTE: This custard may be prepared up to 24 hours before it is served.

Home-Made Yoghurt

Makes 1 litre (1³/₄ pints)

Working time about 20 minutes

Total time: about 3 hours and 20 minutes

Per 1/4 litre (8 fl oz): Calories 230, Protein 13g, Cholesterol
20mg, Total fat 5g, Saturated fat 3g, Sodium 225mg

90 g/3 oz *dried skimmed milk*
1 litre/1³/₄ pint *semi-skimmed milk*
3 tbsp *live plain low-fat yoghurt*

Combine the dried milk and the liquid milk, stirring until the dried milk is completely dissolved. Gently heat the milk until it registers between 43° and 47°C (110° and 115°F) on a sugar thermometer, then remove it from the heat. Stir a little of the warm milk into the yoghurt to temper it, then add the yoghurt to the remaining warm milk. Gently stir the mixture until it is smooth; pour it into two clean 1/2 litre (16 fl oz) jars. Cover the jars tightly and put them in a warm place— on top of your refrigerator for example; 32°C (90°F) is ideal—for 3 to 5 hours.

To test the yoghurt for doneness, tilt one of the jars; the liquid whey should have separated from the solid curd. Press the curd with your finger—it should be firm. If the yoghurt is still semi-liquid, return the jar to the warm place until the curd sets. Pour off the whey, then cover the jars and store them in the refrigerator.

Sliced Watermelon Sorbet

Serves 16

Working time: about 20 minutes

Total time: 4 to 6 hours (includes chilling)

Calories 90, Protein 1g, Cholesterol 0mg, Total fat 1g,
Saturated fat 0g, Sodium 3mg

1 *watermelon (about 3.5 kg/8 lb)*
200 g/7 oz *caster sugar*
2¹/₂ tbsp *fresh lemon juice*
145 g/5 oz *fresh blueberries*

Halve the watermelon lengthwise. Scoop out all the flesh and put it into a large bowl. Select the more attractive half of the watermelon to use for serving; discard the other half. Cut the watermelon half crosswise into slices about 2.5 cm (1 inch) thick. Reassemble the slices so that the watermelon shell appears intact, and freeze it until it is rock-hard and the slices are firmly stuck together. (In order for the slices to cohere, it may be necessary to prop the shell in place during freezing.)

Purée the watermelon flesh in several batches in a blender or food processor, then press it through a sieve to filter out the seeds. Measure the strained fruit; there should be about 1.75 litres (3 pints). (If you have more or less fruit, increase or decrease the amount of sugar accordingly by 2 tablespoons per ¹/₄ litre/8 fl oz of fruit.) Stir the sugar and lemon juice into the strained fruit, then freeze the mixture. No matter which freezing method you select, do not stir the blueberries into the watermelon sorbet until the end of its freezing period.

When the melon shell is frozen solid, fill it with the blueberry-studded sorbet, smoothing the top so the final result will resemble a freshly cut watermelon half. Freeze the assembly until it is solid throughout—at least 2 hours.

Present the watermelon intact. Using the precut lines as a guide, cut the watermelon into slices.